The Circle of Grace

from

The Brotherhood of Light

1/05

*For Georgina,
a Child of Light!*

Edna G. Frankel

EDNA G. FRANKEL

— SARA —

How to Clear Pain & Stress—The Way to Regain & Maintain Health

A Brotherhood Press Book
www.beyondreiki.com
Printed in the United States of America
Cover Art and Design by Elyse Stein Meyerson
ISBN 0-9746415-0-2

Many of the chapters in this book were previously published in
different forms by *Sedona Journal of Emergence!*

Library of Congress Cataloging-in-Publication Data
Frankel, Edna G., 1954 -
Self Help, Stress Relief, Meditation, Holistic Health, Natural Healing,
Metaphysics, Spirituality, Channeled Work.

Dedication

I dedicate this book to Spirit,
For I am just their human scribe.
I dedicate my life to Spirit,
To keep their flow of words alive.

No matter how dark the day may be,
I give thanks for all my blessings.
For my happy, healthy family,
For shelter, food, and yes, our lessons.

It is not enough to just survive,
For all you souls seeking completion.
When I look into your eyes,
I see you, too, are on a mission.

Join me on this journey through Life,
Make each day an easy glide!
Release all sorrow and claim your joy,
For Spirit will always guide and provide.

Sara
9/30/2003

Acknowledgments

I would like to thank all the people who have supported my efforts to create this work. To my dear Reiki friends and students, from whom I learned a lot. To my dear family, who put up with a lot! To my dear editor, Hazel Dawkins, whose tireless talent and keen vision helped me manifest my first book. To all my dear readers, whose e-mails, letters and phone calls kept me going through the most difficult times. And to my dear Bros, without whose whispered words of encouragement I would never have made it this far.

The energy and wisdom of many, many souls are in this work. To All, I give thanks.

I Am, in All Love, Sara

Contents

Introduction

Thoughts from the Brothers About Time and Dimensionality

We feel that earth fully ascended to the fourth dimension (4D) as of the month of May in your year 2000. At that time occurred a "heavenly arrangement" of all planets in your solar system into one long line. This gravitational pull created your "slingshot" from the third to the fourth dimension (3D to 4D). There are many references in this work to the different dimensions of reality on earth; we offer the following explanation so that you will have better understanding as you read the text.

Most of humanity is still unaware of the higher realms and lives in 3D. To those of you reading this page, we say you are now in 4D, and have been since May 2000. Your goal in the ascension process is to access the fifth dimension (5D) and above, where we work and reside. So, when we speak of your world in general and of your past history, we will refer to your existence as 3D. When we speak of the population's current transition, we will call it 3–4D. Since the earth has raised her vibratory rate to 4D, we will call your current Now time 4D. Please understand that these gradual steps are designed to help you evolve without risking any harm to you.

For those of you awakened and aware, working with us in the Circle of Grace raises you into the 4–5D level of transition.

Mastering each dimensional frequency shift makes you a student of the next dimension, so your transition from 4D–5D is actually rising from 4–5D to 5–6D. Your final shift to 6–7D is beyond the scope of this text, but we'll give you a hint: Choosing to go beyond that point will depend on whether or not you choose to keep your body.

Confused yet? We're not done!

We will remind you in this text, time and again, that all dimensions reside in the same space, separated only by levels of vibratory frequency. Since your physical sensory input has always been plugged into 3D, that is all you have known. As you seek higher consciousness, your awareness will expand to include sensory input from those higher levels of existence. Your new "comfort zone," once you finish shifting with the earth, will probably be 5D. Though we endeavor to keep this information within your "linearity framework of reference," know that once you reach 5D and beyond, you cannot keep counting the higher dimensions in numerical order. Why? Because the rules of linearity no longer apply!

While you see each dimension as having specific physical parameters, we see the dimensions as different states of consciousness that can be accessed by meshing with those specific vibratory parameters. For your 3–4D range of awareness to expand beyond your physical understanding into our broader non-physical understanding, we offer here a brief physical explanation.

What defines each dimension? The variables that affect the total vibrational range of existence in that space. 3D has three variables: Height, width and depth. These parameters have formed and limited your awareness of physical reality for thousands of years. Once you become aware that there are other variables at play around you, it will become easier to understand that there are other dimensions, and therefore realities, around you as well.

When you move into 4D, what change do you add? The variable added is *time*.

"What?" you say. "Time is constant! It never changes! It defines our past, present and future! It is beyond our control! It controls us! To think that we can affect time, or change it in any way, is crazy!"

Dear ones, in his time, Columbus was called crazy for daring to think that the world was not flat. If he had succumbed to societal pressures, then human history would have been very different! Indeed, there are many cases recorded in your history of events that ultimately expanded the human consciousness but came at great cost to those humans brave enough to deny the limitations of their time (chuckle). Now you have reached a point in your evolution where we can say, yes, time is one of your limitations!

For you see, time exists as rigid in 3D to give structure to your duality. As you rise up in the dimensions, you will leave linear time behind you. Time is only constant in 3–4D, a line on which you stand that defines your past, present and future. In 4D you will begin to notice that time is not rigid, it speeds up and slows down depending on your awareness of it. From our perspective, time is a circle with no beginning and no end. It is another variable that defines our existence in the higher realms. We call it Now time, and will speak often about "living in the Now." Here we say, Now time is all time, where all is happening at once, and therefore time is open to us to enter and exit as we will.

At first, this concept will be difficult for you to understand. Since we are dealing with difficult concepts, we offer you a similar paradigm to study: All dimensions reside in the same space, separated only by levels of energetic frequency. As all time is Now, so are all the dimensions together as one. You will come to understand this as your current reality expands into the full bloom of 4D, and you still deal with many people who are in 3D. Each dimension expands to include the next! Indeed, they already exist in eternal space, waiting for you to raise your frequency to match the next level. In the text, we will often repeat that 3D and 4D are included in 5D, and so on up the scale.

You already know the parameters of 3D. Now that you are in 4D, you are sensing an expansion of energy around you and within you. You are becoming sensitive to refined levels of stimuli and will inevitably realize that you are becoming psychic, telepathic and empathic. 4D is the psychic expansion corridor between 3D and 5D. In 4D, the Veil of Forgetfulness begins to thin, letting in glimpses of the higher realms.

What happens when you reach 5D? The separation of duality will be gone, linear time will be gone, the veil will be gone, and you will reach wholeness. Wholeness is Oneness with Spirit. You will intimately know your eternal selves and still have much time left to play on this beautiful planet earth. What a wondrous journey lies ahead for you! We are here, directions at the ready, to facilitate your transition from the limited humans that you were to the eternal Be-ings that you truly are.

This book you hold in your hands is your roadmap Home.
Do you follow?
We hope you will.

We are, in All Love, The Brotherhood of Light.

[Channeled January 2003]

Section One

Learning The Circle of Grace Process

Chapter One

The Physical Body

G reetings, dear ones, from the Brotherhood of Light. We are your ancient guardians, the Order of Melchizedek, the spiritual caretakers of humanity. We work in many ways, at many levels, to help humanity evolve to the next octave of consciousness, to the next dimension of potential reality. We come before the Veil of Forgetfulness in your time Now to offer you a new, yet very old way of maintaining health in the human body. We await you in full force, to bring you gracefully through the window of "energetic opportunity" in this pivotal span of human history. We say to you, simply:

> Let us help you to evolve
> To the higher levels of Love.
> Let us teach you how to heal,
> And in healing, Be-come real.

Dear ones, we await you, each in his or her own time, to reach inward and upward for healing. There you will find us waiting, and there you will have your proof that God exists. Once you know, down to your bones, that we are with you, then you will rise into the I Am energy. Your power will be boundless, as will your compassion and your understanding.

Healing your body will heal all of your lives. Heal all the layers of your total Be-ing, and rejoin us in the True Reality Of Spirit. *It is time to remember who You are.*

The Circle of Grace is a simple exercise that heals you at all levels. At the same time that it releases pain and stress, it replenishes your body with new energy. It is a process that occurs naturally in your aura while you sleep—it is how the human body clears itself.

Join in this process with your awareness and our guidance, and learn to heal yourself.

THE BROTHERHOOD HEALING PRAYER

If you wish, light a candle or some incense to help focus your senses. Then, *speak aloud* your desire to have a healing session with us in this four-part prayer:

Call upon Father/Mother God, Creator of all that is, was, and ever will be, to join you in the healing session.

Call upon your favorite Ascended Masters, guides, angels, and religious figure(s), whomever you hold dear, to join you in the healing session.

Call upon us, the Brotherhood Of Light, to join you in the healing session.

Call upon your own soul, or Higher Self, to join you and guide the healing session.

Do it out loud. Say the words, say how you feel, say what you choose and what you release (i.e., I choose total health, I release my illness). The vibration of your voice brings the idea, the sentiment, the desire into the fruition of your 3rd and 4th dimensions, the dimensions of material and materialization. Due to the parameters of your free will zone, we must wait for your spoken intent before we can begin. Why? Saying the Healing Prayer gives us permission to join with you, merging 4D and 5D so that we may interact in your space at the physical level.

Do you follow?

We hope you will.

The Circle of Grace clears the meridians of the body via the meridians of the aura. Both come into play when you do the work of clearing your energetic system. Once you get accustomed to doing the Circle of Grace, you will gain mastery over your own healing. You will learn to tap into the Circle whenever you need energy and learn to release pain as it comes in so that it does not accumulate, clog your meridians, and make you sick.

The Circle of Grace is your natural birthright—the physical link to your inner divine power. We offer to work with you to bring you into full self-mastery. What is full self-mastery? Having control over the health of your total Be-ing and the use of your energy, at all levels. Then you will begin to create your own future at a level where dreams, indeed, can and do come true.

EXPANDING YOUR FRAMEWORK OF REFERENCE

Successful healing for a person must occur on three levels: physical (medical), emotional-mental (psychological), and spiritual (auric). When science and spirituality finally meet and merge, healing will become a simple process.

Your biggest obstacle to healing is thinking that your physical body is your entire being. It is only half of you! It is the physical core into which your other half—your auric self, or energetic self—is entwined. Modern medicine does not honor the other half of each patient that is invisible because it is invisible. But your aura is invisible only to your senses, which are anchored in the 3rd dimension. Think of the concept of a dog whistle, which is an octave above man's range of hearing. Blow on that whistle and you hear nothing. Yet your dog comes running because he has heard your call. In the same way, your auric or energetic self has been beyond the range of your 3D senses, but that does not mean your aura does not exist—it only means that you have not been able to see, feel, hear or interact with your auric self, the way you do with your physical self.

Once you begin to flower into the 4D sensory range, all of that will change!

When medicine understands and accepts that it only focuses on half of a human being, people will begin to create instruments capable of tuning into the interdimensional levels of a person—measuring the aura, and the level of health or disease carried in that electromagnetic field. Indeed, you have begun:

Electroencephalograms, or EEGs, measure brain waves or energetic brain activity. Your electrocardiograms, or EKG tests, measure the energetic pulse of your hearts. These are both auric functions that are now essential to proper diagnosis.

Once you begin to explore the aura's form and functions, you will finally understand the full workings of the total human being. This will move your medical knowledge forward greatly and eradicate many current illnesses, especially in the areas of mental, hormonal and immune imbalances. *You keep looking in the body for physical ways to fix these systems; we say, look instead for the electromagnetic imbalances in the auric field. There you will find the system controls, and you will find what to fix!*

You already have Kirlian photographic equipment, which shows the energetic field of any living subject. Once you develop similar equipment in the form of movie cameras, you will be able to track the movement of etheric energy, and truly show the impact of energetic lightworkers on the human energetic system. This new equipment will ultimately provide invaluable diagnostic information for the medical community. You will learn to find and clear auric blockages, or "stress pockets," that are magnetized to the body's electromagnetic field. Once you release the spiritual dis-ease, it will not manifest as a disease in the body's physical core. This is what we offer to teach you. Learning and using the Circle of Grace will bring mastery of healing and self-empowerment into the human consciousness more quickly!

Doctors now agree that all illness is a result of stress in your lives. By the time they are presented with an illness, they can only track it back to where it appeared in the body and then label it according to which area, system or organ has been affected. Without alleviating the circumstances in your life that caused the stress in the first place, you will have either a failed or incomplete healing, or a temporary remission. Release that stress pocket and the situation that caused it, and the physical symptoms will withdraw from the body.

Many hands-on modalities are being developed and fine-tuned to release stress from the aura before it causes a physical illness. Reiki is the most well known as a foundational modality that uses universal energy to clear and heal the aura. There are many other wonderful energetic modalities coming into your awareness now. Plus, there are older modalities like acupuncture, shiatsu and reflexology, which work directly on the physical meridians to clear blockages. These are all tools, dear ones, energetic healing tools to apply to the Circle of Grace clearing process.

Once an illness has manifested in the body, it is more difficult to clear.

Heal the damaged aura, and you will not get sick.

People get sick in one of two ways—either a disease establishes itself in the region of the non-functional chakra, or too much stress overloads the system, which breaks down at the site of your genetic predisposition to illness. By this we mean inherited diseases such as cancer, diabetes, etc. Very often, the best way to treat acute disease is to have it cut out (as in the case of cancerous tumors), or attack the infection with antibiotics (like in pneumonia or ulcers), or set the broken bone with osteopathic knowledge and then cast the area. We are all in favor of using the modern technology available today—doctors perform an invaluable service to humanity.

But what if you were to go to the doctor and say, "Dear Sir, I have pain in this region of my body, which is invisible to you. Please help me!" That is the situation faced by most modern healers, scientific or holistic. The scientific mind-set ignores what it cannot see or measure.

The holistic mind-set works on wherever the pain may be, and tracks it back to its true source—damage in the auric field. The hands-on healers among you work mostly blind, for their 4D senses are just beginning to register information from the aura, which vibrates in the higher dimensions. Many holistic practitioners get "diagnostic impressions" in their hands and can feel their way through to righting the damage that has been done. This is also, in a true physical sense, reading the aura. Some of you are now developing inner sight, or soon will, which is another gift that grows with your expansion into your new 4-5D sensory range!

THE VEIL OF FORGETFULNESS

Your body is an incredible conglomeration of organs and systems that form a symphony of life essence known as humanity. Once you have a clearer understanding of how the aura interacts with its physical core, you will soon realize that the aura is as complex and as miraculous as the body that supports it. How could it not be?

The biggest challenge to healing is the fact that you cannot yet see or interact with your energetic selves. Since it is not part of your awareness, you cannot feel your aura, much less heal it. Please understand here that your left brain connects you to and directs your physical body. Your right brain connects you to and directs the etheric layers that comprise your aura.

Why do you feel one and not the other? Because of the Veil of Forgetfulness. The right brain houses your slumbering connection to Spirit. We say "slumbering" because the Veil is a spiritual mechanism that blocks you from knowledge of other dimensions, of life before birth and after death. It was designed to block out the higher levels of your awareness in order to keep you focused on each current life in the 3rd dimension, and thus ensure karmic reincarnation.

You do not remember that you are Eternal!

Due to the Veil, you have had no conscious knowledge of anything other than the 3rd dimension. That is why you have been in constant, concrete communication with your physical body yet have not been able to exchange a word or thought with your aura. Even if you manage to influence or touch your aura, you cannot hear the answer in clear words—the information you receive is a flow of emotions, feeling good, bad or indifferent to every situation. This is your aura communicating with you!

Learn to use this "intuition," as you call it, to assess and weigh every emotion that arises as an answer to your current situation. Realize that your aura, by virtue of being in layers of higher dimensions, sees and knows more than your physical senses that are keyed only into the 3rd dimension. As you flower into the broader sensory range of 4D, you will understand that the Veil is thinning! Once you shift from 4D into

5D, you will outgrow the need for separation from Spirit and outgrow the limitations of the Veil Of Forgetfulness altogether.

When you are awake, the Veil is down. When you are asleep, the Veil rises and you are free to link with Spirit. You already know that while the body needs a certain amount of sleep each day, your mind never rests. In dreams, the mind continues to function. For those of you doing astral work, the Spirit aspect of your being continues its work during dream time, letting the body rest. Why does the body need rest? To clear itself of physical trauma and emotional baggage, both old and new. The stress that you pick up daily, most of it inherent in your fast-paced, complex society, must be released first. Then you can access and clear the deeper layers of chronic pain from old wounds, including past life issues.

How does your body accomplish this self-healing? By clearing and replenishing the energy in your nervous system while you sleep. By the activation of what we call the Circle of Grace. Forgive the long introduction, but the framework of reference is much more intricate than the actual work. Once you understand in your mind and body how this clearing takes place, you will be able to activate it at any time you wish, to regain and maintain your health.

You have the power to heal yourself. There is a clearing mechanism already present in your body! If you will, let us teach you how to use it.

Dominant and Nondominant, Right and Left: A moment is needed here to explain dominant and nondominant sides of the body. The dominant side can be seen as which hand you write with. If you are ambidextrous, try to remember which hand you used as a small child, first introduced to writing. If you were left-handed but were forced at school to write with your right hand, your body is still left-side dominant. If you don't remember, watch which hand you use to reach with, to eat with, to hold your toothbrush—all these actions speak to dominance of one side over another. An energetic healer or Reiki practitioner can also determine the natural polarity of the body. This is very important to ascertain, since the normal, healthy Circle of Grace enters the dominant foot and exits from the nondominant hand and foot.

This dominance aspect of the body also defines which hand is positive in hands-on healing, and which hand is negative. This relates to the holistic healer: Your dominant hand is the positive flow of energy and your nondominant hand is the negative flow. Together, they form a closed circuit by which energy is channeled through the body of the receiver. For the sake of clarity and brevity, we will refer to the dominant side as being the right side, which is more common amongst you.

For left-side dominant people, please understand that your approach is simply the reverse, or mirror image, of what follows. In the normal Circle of Grace pattern, your receiving foot is the left, and you will feel energy rise up your left side. Your releasing foot is the right, and you will feel more clearing occur down the right side. For those who are unsure, you can sense during the Circle of Grace which foot is receiving (it will feel like it is being pushed back and upright) and which foot is releasing (it will feel pulled forward and down). You can also tell which side is dominant by tracking the path of the release, for it will flow down the nondominant side, and that will be the side in which you may feel more of the energetic movement.

WHY THE CIRCLE OF GRACE WORKS

The Circle of Grace clears your nervous system. Your nervous system is embedded in your body, yes, but it also exists throughout your aura, or electromagnetic field, in a holographic pattern (as are all of your "physical" systems!). What you call the nervous system is inside you, but its reflected pattern in the aura you call the body's "energetic meridians." Do you see now, how both are really one and the same? Stimulating any level of this system, physical or auric, will cause it to release. The body clears itself automatically at night, when you are asleep. For those of you who wake up each day with pain in the same spots, those are your chronic meridian blockages that interfere with the energy flow. In our healing sessions together, we can help you clear those spots, those aches and pains, and cumulative stress as well.

To heighten understanding, know that the energy meridians traced by the Chinese over 3,000 years ago for acupuncture are in reality an overlay of your nervous system. That is why acupuncture works so well in accelerating healing and reducing swelling—it clears the energy meridians appropriate to the damage, allowing the Circle of Grace to flow, which aids the body to heal itself. For those with a fear of needles, there are many other hands-on modalities that help quicken meridian release. Explore shiatsu, jin shin jyutsu, foot reflexology, acupressure and the many forms of therapeutic massage that help stimulate blockages to clear.

So, the aura sustains the total body's life flow by circulating universal energy through its physical core and all of its etheric layers. The nervous system is to the aura what the (blood) circulatory system is to the body. While blood is meant to flow in only one direction, the nervous system is much more versatile, as shown in the upcoming section on the Circle of Grace patterns. The nervous system also has a flow—a constant intake of universal energy—that can go in any direction it needs to clear itself. The purpose of this flow is to collect stress and pain in your *total being*, both physical and etheric, and release it so that it does not accumulate.

This process also energizes the body as it is clearing. How? Universal energy is food to your aura. No matter where the Circle of Grace begins, as it releases pain it also feeds new, clean energy into your system at the same time. Your nervous system is a closed-pressure system; when one end releases, the other end automatically rebalances the pressure by taking in an equal amount of new, clean energy. ***Whenever you do this exercise, no matter which flow pattern arises, you clear and replen - ish the energy in your system at the same time.***

Pain and stress are the waste products of your body's energetic functions. Your nervous system is designed to "flush away" the waste from all the layers of your total being. The universal energy that runs through your nervous system absorbs your pain in a magnetic way. The pain literally melts into the golden flow, which becomes dark and tainted as it progresses through your body.

Imagine this flow akin to oil in your cars—the oil keeps everything running smoothly, but gets dirty with the byproducts of released energy. You have determined how long your cars can run efficiently before the oil gets so dirty that it needs to be changed. We say to you here: *Your bodies require "oil changes" much more frequently than your automobiles!*

WHY PEOPLE GET SICK

Here is a concept important to assimilate: Pain and stress have physical properties of mass and density that exist in the higher dimensions of your body—in your aura. Because the energetic meridians are intricately tied to the physical nervous system meridians, pain and stress also exist inside you as physical objects. While your body must deal with them as causing painful pressure, your senses cannot track what is happening to you from the 3rd dimension. You cannot yet see these "pockets of pain energy," just as you do not yet see your own auras, so you discount their existence.

Even though you cannot see your pain, did you ever wonder why you feel it so clearly? Because pain is as real and concrete as your body is, and its presence causes painful pressure inside you. Once you realize that pain and stress are solid objects as real as your skin, muscles and bones, you will reach a new perspective on how to get clear and stay balanced. In regards to explaining the phenomenon of pain, your language is limited— you have only one word for pain! It must be qualified in different ways to express what type of pain you are feeling.

For example, stress is actually low-level pain. You have begun to understand this connection, for your medical community now realizes that all illness is caused by stress. Stress is pain, and the accumulation of too much pain in your nervous system results in blockage of the cleansing flow of energy that is meant to circulate to keep your total Be-ing healthy.

We shall, in this work, use your language to help explain the Circle of Grace. Think about the expression, "You're getting on my last nerve!" What does it mean in energetic terms? That your clearing mechanism, your nervous system, is so clogged with old, tainted energy that there is no room left in it to absorb any more stress. What happens when the system gets overloaded? Again, pain is a physical object in your body; it has to go somewhere. Where does it go? Where do you stuff your pain away? What are the chronic weak spots in your body that rear up and hurt when you get "stressed out"? Those are the areas in which your energetic meridians are blocked, causing the overflow of pain to settle in your tissues, muscles and bones. Since it does not belong there, it causes physical pressure, which you recognize as chronic pain.

That is how blockages are formed, dear ones, and these blockages bring the Circle of Grace flow to a complete stop. Once the flow is cut off, there is no way for the body to clear itself in that area. The body switches to alternate meridians in order to release pressure in the entire system. The more alternate routes it is forced to take, the weaker the flow becomes. The weaker the flow becomes, the less "life force" you have to get you through each day. If you have chronic pain that eludes a diagnosis and your doctor can find nothing wrong, you may well find relief in doing the Circle of Grace in healing sessions with us and learning how to clear your auric blockages.

You already know that illness strikes in one of two ways, either in the area of the emotional blockages or through the weak spots in your genetic make-up (i.e., the inherited tendencies of illness in families, like cancer or heart disease). We offer you this exercise in hopes of expanding your awareness of how your bodies work, and how to stay healthy.

You do not need to succumb to illness. With the Circle of Grace, you can heal yourself, keep your body healthy, live longer and have a better quality of life.

You can carry etheric damage for a long, long time before it invades the physical core of your Be-ing. If you regularly clear your auric self of pain, illness will not physically manifest in your body.

Do you follow?

We hope you will.

The lynch pin to this exercise is *active meditation*. Through the quieting of the mind and the inward focus of attention, you can feel this miracle of self-clearing happen naturally in your body. We will ask that you focus on the energy moving inside you, and *track out loud for us where it goes.* If you argue here that you do not meditate and have no intent to do so, please know that this is a meditation focused on body aware-ness, not just trying to relax and not think. If you don't want to meditate at all, see it as an "active relaxation" session! You can also activate the Circle of Grace to clear yourself as you are falling asleep, resting, reading or watching television.

Do you recognize the axiom, "In prayer you speak to God, in meditation you listen to God"? In saying the Healing Prayer to connect with us, you are speaking to God about what you need. As you slide into the Circle of Grace, you switch to listening and feeling our presence and gentle ministrations. Thus, this process works in perfect balance—giving and receiving. Give us your time and your faith, and you will receive God's Grace.

Our goal is to teach all human beings how to heal them-selves. In our healing sessions together, we focus on clearing and balancing all layers of your total Be-ing. Please understand that learning and implementing the Circle of Grace is crucial for your imminent evolution; we encourage you to use this exercise whenever you feel the need to clear and energize your-self. Once you have full awareness of this process, you can will it to begin any time you wish.

But the real, deep-down work we do with each person in healing sessions is a major part of your metaphysical progress—remember that our session time together is crucial, as we heal on all levels, though you may still only sense the physical realm. In other words, yes, do the Circle whenever you need to for physical clearing and rebalancing, but please do not forget to schedule time to work with us at the conceptual level, as well.

HOW THE CIRCLE OF GRACE WORKS

You must open your jaw to activate the Circle of Grace. Your jaw is your on-off switch. When your jaw is clenched, the meridians will not release! When the jaw joints are relaxed, the meridians flow freely.

The Circle of Grace flows in different patterns through the body, depending on the needs of the person at that particular time. ***Most people begin with the blocked patterns.*** These different flows are all appropriate to healing. You will discover that your body often switches back and forth between patterns, doing what it needs at that moment in the following ways:

Fully Blocked Pattern: This pattern engages when the nervous system needs full release. The body clears from the head down on both sides simultaneously. Imagine a golden cloud of universal energy above your head. As it descends around your body and into the top of your head, the Circle of Grace begins to flow (your energetic meridians start to release). Remember to keep your jaw open. The Circle flows down both sides of the neck, then down both arms and legs at the same time, releasing through the joints and chakras of the hands and feet.

Alternating Blocked Pattern: The body shifts into this pattern as internal pressure eases. Beginning from the top down on both sides, the Circle of Grace energy will flow down the arms and out the hands, then the body switches to releasing down the legs and out the feet (top half releases, then bottom half, then top half again, etc.).

Normal Pattern: This pattern arises when your meridians are free-flowing. Entering at the dominant foot and hand, new energy rises up the dominant side of the body, circles around the head, pushing old, spent energy ahead of it as it descends down the nondominant side to release from hand and foot.

Blockage Reversal: You can intend for the Circle of Grace clearing to go in any direction you choose. Rather than release through the entire body, you can imagine the flow start from the site of pain and move directly to the nearest exit. Beginning at the site of blockage, the Circle will reverse towards the nearest hand or foot, to release pain. For example, blockage in the right elbow will release down the forearm and out the right hand.

HOW TO DO THE CIRCLE OF GRACE EXERCISE

When studying the Circle of Grace, lie down with spine straight and arms at your sides. You can progress to sitting, but it is easier to begin practicing flat on your back. Place pillows beneath your head and knees (to prevent lower back strain). Do not cross your arms or legs, since physical pressure short-circuits the meridians and the flow may momentarily cease. In that regard, it is important to wear loose, comfortable clothing (preferably natural fibers) and remove your shoes. If that is not possible, then loosen whatever you can—belts, bras, shoes. Any constriction on the physical body causes restriction of your energetic meridians, just as any injury, illness or surgery to the physical body also causes damage to your energetic structures.

It is vital to open your jaw, or unclench it at least, so that the energy may flow through that double joint. Your jaw is the on-off switch that starts and stops the Circle of Grace. When your jaw is tense, your whole body is tense! When you relax your jaw, the body follows suit.

A note for people who have physical damage in and around the jaw: The jaw joints or temporal-mandibular joints (TMJ) are the only joints in the body that work in tandem, as a pair. All of your other joints, both fixed and moving, are single joints that work alone. Your lower jaw is suspended like a see-saw. If one jaw joint is damaged, the other joint eventually suffers damage by force of misaligned pressure. Even if only one side hurts, always clear both sides!

For TMJ sufferers, use a high pillow beneath your head so that your jaw naturally points down, then drop your jaw open to let the meridians flow. If you lie too flat and your lower jaw slides back instead of forward, this position will cause more pain rather than relieving what is there. After you relax the jaw, tip your head left, then right (a small motion is sufficient) to activate the meridian flows. If your mind wanders away from the exercise, merely open your jaw and tip your head again to either side to reactivate the release.

Being focused on your breathing also helps to keep the process moving, and gives your left brain busy work, as well! We offer here an elementary version of yogic breathing, which you can modify to suit your lung capacity. The key is to breathe slowly and deliberately, so as not to hyperventilate. Breathe in (to a comfortable count between 1–7), pause (1–3), breathe out (1–7), pause (1–3). If you have trouble sustaining two pauses, try breathing in, breathing out, then pause once after you exhale. *Each pause presses down on your meridians and cre - ates a wave of release down the body.*

Dear ones, we are recreating here the cadence of your breathing during sleep, which actually pushes the meridians to release in slow, pulsing waves. By consciously controlling your breathing, you will learn to direct your body's internal cleansing mechanism. Between this focused breathing and your speaking out loud to us what you feel during the session, do you see why we call the Circle of Grace an "active" meditation? Your left brain has plenty to do while we are working with you. Through this process, you will develop the ability to control your thinking, your breathing, your clearing and your healing!

Once you are comfortable with the Circle of Grace exercise, you can add this refinement to your meditation: breathe up the right side, pause as it circles around your head, then breathe down the left side and pause again. See each inhalation as a wave of clean, golden energy flowing in and up your right side, and see each exhalation as a gray, cloudy wave flowing down and out your left side. In this way, you will learn to efficiently and effectively use this exercise as part of your routine body maintenance.

Now how does the Circle of Grace feel? That is as individual as you are, yet the sensations always follow the same patterns. For those lucky people who are relatively healthy and balanced, you will not get the same intensity of sensations as someone who is ill. You may still feel a "flow" circulating, sometimes only slight sensations in the left leg as pressure leaves your system. Many people report this as feeling a cool liquid sliding down inside the left leg.

Or you may only feel a tingling in your fingers and toes when you do the exercise. Some people will feel nothing at all, yet find that they have much more energy to get them through the day.

In either case, the Circle of Grace is working to clear and energize you. Remember that your body naturally clears itself in this way every night, no matter what position you choose to sleep in. If you do wake up with left-side pain, massage it down and out your arm or leg. If you are energetically attuned, work above the blockage, then move it down and out. Often, just being conscious of this process is enough to set it in motion. Know that as fresh energy enters your system, it is naturally pushing ahead of it old, spent energy from the day before that is now laced with pain. That is why, by the time the Circle crests around your head and comes back down again (in the normal pattern), you may feel the energy change into a sensation of pressure or an achy feeling, even sometimes a sharp line as it slides down and out.

Know that these sensations are transient, do not be afraid of feeling pain in this process. What you are feeling is the passage of the pain, an echo of its progress that tells you of its path. For those of you who do not pick up any sensations, focus on the energizing aspect of the Circle of Grace. A half-hour of this exercise in the morning will give you much energy for the day, making you feel younger and stronger. Again, this is a self-correcting system that works with or without your conscious mind in the driver's seat. Once you become aware of this process, you can actively participate in your own self-healing, from clearing meridian blocks to clearing headaches, back pain or any pain anywhere.

WORKING WITH ENERGETIC BLOCKAGES

Fully Blocked Pattern: *Remember that the Circle of Grace can run in any direction that your body needs at the time.* For those of you who are totally blocked, the direction of the Circle will begin from the top down, using both sides of the body to release pain and stress. See it as a golden cloud or shower descending into and around you. Feel it enter the top of your head, go down both sides of your neck, then flow down both arms and legs at the same time. (This full-body releasing will occur at your direction once you gain familiarity with the Circle of Grace exercise.)

Your body naturally splits the releasing flow to other meridians to decrease the pressure in each individual meridian. The top of each shoulder is where this fork occurs. Pain from the armpits up usually exits down both arms at once, and pain from the armpits down usually clears down both sides and legs at once. Here is an overview of the major meridian flows that your body utilizes to clear your nervous system:

At the shoulder, the energy divides into different meridians to ease the internal pressure. Two meridians flow down each arm, one going down the back of the arm over the elbow and one going down the inner arm. If there is a heavy flow, the energy will also split at the shoulder and go down the torso, again on both sides if the body chooses to release on both dominant and nondominant sides. The legs each have four meridians, two parallel on the inside and outside of the thigh, and two centered above and beneath the knees. The meridian below the knee is an extension of the sciatic nerve trunk, a major path of release running straight down the back of the leg, from lower back to heel.

The release will occur in pulsing waves of pressure, which you will learn to control through focused breathing. This can be a fascinating process, for those who seek inner knowledge or higher and deeper levels of meditation. Once you become adept at doing the Circle of Grace, you will eventually release down the front or back of your body, in waves of pressure that exit at the feet. You will learn how to release lower back pain down the back of both legs, through the sciatic nerve trunks and out the feet. You will be able to drain a headache down both arms and out your hands.

Do not feel overwhelmed by all of these details; simply begin by saying the Healing Prayer, tell us your intent and how much time you have for the session. Let us work with your physical body while you rest. The patterns will arise time and again, as we show you how to clear yourself of pain and stress. *There is no set pattern that indicates total health.* The needs of your body are ever-changing, and the flexibility of the releasing patterns allow you to be in charge of your energy level and your overall health, no matter what your needs of the moment may be.

Alternating Blocked Pattern: Once your system has
been partially cleared, your upper and lower meridians will
begin taking turns—you will feel the arms release, then that
will cease and your legs will release for a while. This alternating
pattern will continue until enough pressure has been relieved
inside the nervous system for your body to assume the normal
Circle of Grace pattern.

An example of the alternating blocked pattern: To clear
headaches, you can run the Circle of Grace down both arms at
the same time. *Open your jaw* to open the head/neck meridians,
and tip your head left (a tiny motion will do). This activates
the left meridian flow. Then tip your head to the right, to activate that side. Keeping your jaw open, you will feel the
headache actually course down your neck on both sides and go
down your arms in light waves of pressure. If it is a very deep
headache, you may feel waves flowing down your whole body,
with the headache exiting via the arms, and the nausea flowing
down the legs, taking turns to release. If it slows down, another good way to activate the meridians is by flexing your hand
(or foot) back up against the wrist (or ankle) joint, as if making
a stopping motion. That will tug on the meridians from the
exit point to stimulate release. Remember to keep focused on
your breathing to keep the meridians flowing!

Normal Pattern: When using the Circle of Grace for self-
maintenance, know that once you say the Healing Prayer out
loud, lie down and focus on your breathing, you will feel the
session begin within one or two minutes. The body naturally
releases internal pressure downward via the meridians of the
nervous system to exit points which are the joints and chakras
of the hands and feet. Many of you think that energy leakage
occurs at the joints, and that that is a bad thing. To us, joints
are multi-purpose, and for our purpose here it is to use them
as little doorways by which to release your pain and stress.

For a healthy person, the Circle of Grace begins and ends in
the feet. Your aura draws in universal energy through the right
(or left-dominant) foot chakra and draws it up the right (or
left) side of the body. Once the Circle is fully activated, many
will feel as if your right foot is being pressed up and back,

while your left foot will feel as if it is being pulled forward and down. You will have this sensation even if both feet are in exactly the same position. What you are feeling is the tug and direction of the energy circling through your body.

Those who are sensitive to energy flows will also feel new energy entering their right hand chakra and going up the right arm. Many receivers of Reiki, which provides the "energetic push" for the Circle of Grace to begin, have described this sensation as "champagne bubbles" going up their right leg, while some feel a right-sided "heaviness" as universal energy permeates their system. This energy goes up the right neck meridian through the relaxed jaw joint, over the crown (which starts its own circular pulsing) and back down the left side of the neck.

When the energy reaches the top of the left shoulder it splits into two main meridian trunks, one going down the left arm, and the other going down the left side down to the leg. This new, clean energy is pushing before it waves of "pain" to be released through the left hand and foot chakras. You may feel achy waves of pressure flowing down your left arm/side/leg. You may feel a tiny hot line within your muscles as a blocked meridian is cleared. If the pain gets stuck in a spot, tell us aloud and we will move it down and out. Reiki heat applied above any blockage, plus a small massage to the area down toward the hand or foot, will also loosen and clear the blockage.

Even the focus of your mental intent, without any external help, can clear your meridians if you understand that this is possible. We will teach you how to do this in our healing sessions together. Know that you will feel this circuit of energy working. Know that you can tell it to go where you want, when you want it to, by simply lying down and focusing on the process to turn it on. Yes, there are thousands of meridians and chakras throughout the body, all of which serve multiple purposes. Even the twelve meridians we are describing here have other flows and functions. We are, indeed, keeping the information simple and direct to facilitate your learning how to use the clearing mechanism already within you.

Reverse Blockages: What we described above is the normal flow of energy in a healthy body. If you are ill or have an

injury, know that you can change the direction of this flow to
release pain from the nearest "exit," meaning the hands and
feet. If pain exists on your dominant side, for example in the
right elbow, you can reverse the flow to release pain down your
right forearm and out your right hand. That is a much closer
exit than running the full Circle of Grace up over the head and
down and out the nondominant side. Merely ask us in session
to clear the injury via the closest exit, and we will do so.

For energetic practitioners, know that you can attune the
"exit chakra" and the site of blockage to open them energetically. Then add energy above the blockage and move it down
and out with a gentle stroking motion. If you do not know
how to do energetic attunements, simply make six to nine
counterclockwise circles with your dominant hand above the
area of blockage. Your intent to open and clear that spot will
work just as well!

When clearing multiple blockages, please know that the
one nearest the exit must clear first. For example, if you have a
sprained wrist and an ear infection on the same side, the wrist
pain must be released first or the ear pain will stay blocked
behind it, unable to move.

WORKING IN SESSION WITH THE BROTHERHOOD

You only need to give verbal intent to do the Circle of
Grace and call in the higher help as we described. Then lie
down, and speak to us out loud. Tell us what you want, what
you are tired of, what you wish to heal. *Tell us aloud* if you feel a
blockage, and we will work on releasing it. Some of you will
feel us working, some not. Do not feel bad if you fall asleep;
we sometimes work best when the body is asleep. You have
not missed the healing session! Some of us work at the physical level, while other Brothers work with your higher mind at
the conceptual level. Remember, healing must occur on all levels, not just the physical. Simply tell us at the beginning how
much time you have for the session, and we will keep time for
you (chuckle). You will wake up, much refreshed, an hour later,
or forty-five minutes, or a half hour.

Sometimes you may find yourself weeping (clearing emotional stress), or bathed in waves of tickling energy (energizing the body), or feel your arms and/or legs filling with pressure seeking release. *Tell us aloud* if the process becomes painful, and we will tone down the work. Sometimes the flow gets stuck behind a big joint (hip, knee or elbow) and forms a pocket or blockage that needs to be moved down and out. Also *tell us aloud* if the Circle slows or gets stuck, and where. We will endeavor to move the flow along, guided by your verbal feedback and fueled by your new, conscious awareness of this miraculous process that is built into your body. Do you see why we call this "active meditation"?

Sometimes the bigger pain pocket, the bigger the joint needed to clear it. You may feel pain exit sideways through your wrist or ankle joint. Sometimes the blockage will continue down to the ends of the meridians and exit through your finger or toe joints. It can also exit in between, at the knuckle portion of the hand or the metatarsal area of the foot. Those of you familiar with Eastern knowledge of release points will find that we use many of them!

Again, you don't need to control this process, merely observe out loud how it feels and where it tends to block. Once you become familiar with the Circle of Grace, you can guide the pressure-pain to release directly through your hand and foot chakras. When you've fully learned how to use it, you'll be able to release pain straight down the front and/or back of your body, and out your feet.

For those of you who wake up with pain in your nondominant leg, know that your meridians were not able to fully clear down and out the left foot during the night. For those who are post-operative and have pain on your left side, hip or knee, not near where the surgery occurred, know that too much trauma to your body produced too much internal pressure for the meridians to effectively clear out the non-dominant side.

The doctors will shake their heads and say, "Sorry, we operated on your shoulder, head, torso, etc., and we don't know why your left leg/hip/knee/ankle is hurting. Get some rest, take these pain pills, and it will fade." Yes, that is good advice, because the body at rest naturally performs the Circle of Grace to clear itself. When physical trauma occurs, there is often too big a pain pocket to slide down and out the meridians all at once. Massage also does wonders for painful blockages—remember, a knotted muscle contains a physical mass of pain within it, spilled over from the blocked meridian into the body proper.

Sometimes the body has healed a trauma as much as it can, but years later you still have pain trapped in that area—like a ten-year-old whiplash. It will remain fixed in place until it is energetically "lanced" and drained away. Why? These etheric pockets have physical weight and density in your body, but are simply not visible to you yet in your physical reality.

Imagine trying to shove a banana through a straw. Will it fit? No. Will it go through and out the other end? With patience and repeated force, you might get a trickle of banana out the other end, but most of it will remain squished in your hand and stuck in the straw. Identifying an energetic blockage is a big step towards true health, and realizing the natural path of clearing that blockage is another big step. Once you begin to practice this exercise, you will finally be in full charge of your own healing.

The true beauty of the Circle of Grace is that it clears not only the physical body but your entire energetic Be-ing, including all four layers of the dense body: Physical, Emotional, Mental and Spiritual (PEMS). Your chakra system is the "spine" of your etheric layers, which is why proper clearing and balancing of the chakras creates a condition of health at all levels. Know that each chakra controls a region of the body, plus the organs and systems in that area.

Besides being your body's clearing system, the Circle of Grace also performs another vital function: it constantly re-energizes your body. The Circle is already within you, only you are not aware of it. Once you find it and begin to affect it with your conscious mind, you will become a self-healer at all levels. Your evolutionary progress will gain momentum at all levels!

Remember that the left brain is connected to and directs the physical body, while the right brain is connected to and directs the etheric layers that comprise your aura. Imagination, creativity, courage, faith and many other wonderful human attributes are right brain and, therefore, auric functions. Do you see now why these things are difficult to access? Because your awareness is left-brained and you need to reconnect consciously to your right brain. These attributes exist in all the layers of your multidimensional body, since humans are holographic in design. This holographic concept is reflected all through the Divine Plan, as well. As you rise into 4D awareness and beyond, you will begin to see the interconnections between all things, see the patterns of life ebbing and flowing, and know that you are a part of All That Is.

Through this healing process you will truly, consciously, become a multidimensional Be-ing. Why do we spell it thus? As a trigger word for your higher consciousness: We use the verb "to be" to indicate the full blend of all your aspects, physical and non-physical layers, with a capital letter as homage to your divinity in the same way we pay homage to God and His works. The "-ing" part of the word "Be-ing" indicates the Now aspect of your ascension, in the present tense, children, to remind you to keep hold of that higher perspective in every moment.

The body of work that we offer here reflects the commitment we have made to the Divine Plan. The Brotherhood Of Light is dedicated to teaching humans how to incorporate all the different aspects of their total Be-ing while still in body, and thus gracefully ascend into the higher realms. In order to blend all of your layers into Oneness, those layers must be cleared and balanced first! That is why we are here, to offer our help to you through the Circle of Grace healing process.

We hope that you now understand why meditation requires you to "still" the chatty left brain, which allows you to be open and receptive to consciously reconnecting to the right brain. So do not keep busy trying to squelch thought, for you are thus blocking all thought. Try instead to suspend mundane thought, like a clear TV screen waiting for a transmission, and follow the sensations of the Circle of Grace. Remember this is an active meditation, an exercise in which we hope you will speak to us out loud, and voice your needs through the session.

Some of you are protesting here—I don't meditate. I don't care to. Know that if you are opposed to the very idea of meditation, then don't do it. Call it a visualization, if you prefer. We ask that you lie down anyway, and imagine a golden cloud of energy entering the top of your head and flowing down your body like a shower. ***In the beginning, don't try to choose which pattern to do, allow your body to do what it needs to do.*** Allow your group of Brothers to choose what you need at each session. If you feel the blocked pattern begin, track your golden cloud visualization straight down both sides. If you feel energy enter your dominant side, go up and around your head, then down the nondominant side, visualize your golden cloud following that path. Then see this golden energy surrounding you like a cocoon, permeating every level of your total Be-ing with healing energy.

For those of you who have no time to meditate, you can activate the Circle of Grace as you're falling asleep, and that simple act will augment and intensify the work that the body naturally does at night to clear itself. This can be a very active process or not, depending on your views and needs. Eventually, you will find that every time you lie down to watch television, read a book, or rest, your body will automatically begin clearing! Once the Circle of Grace becomes part of your life, you will make great strides toward full mastery.

If you are still protesting, then we gently ask, do you enjoy getting in your own way? If you are reading this text, you are a seeker of spirituality, of faith, of Oneness. We offer this information to you as an aid "up the ladder" to the next level of human evolution. However you assimilate this data into your life is your choice; whether for yourself or others, this process is in each and every one of you. Seek it, find it, and use it. You will soon shine, brighter and brighter, as you discover and explore your inner world, your God-self, your portion of the I Am All That Is. Our gift to you is one of natural healing, through the Circle of Grace.

Chapter Two

The Emotional Body

In this second chapter, we would like to focus on the emotional body. You all have emotions, to varying degrees, but you do not know how to use them wisely. By this we mean that you have lost their true purpose and cannot, therefore, use emotions with conscious wisdom. In offering an "energetic" perspective on how your bodies work, and how the universal laws affect your expanding reality, we hope to show you that "wisdom" is already within you—you are simply not conscious of it yet!

As energetic beings, your bodies are layered in holographic patterns that are much more intricate than your current knowledge has defined. For the purpose of our work together, we focus here on the dense etheric body, comprised of physical, emotional, mental and spiritual aspects (PEMS). These layers are distinct and can work independently, but "who you are" is a constant expression of the unique meld of each human being, with all aspects working together to form a cohesive whole. The more you have understanding of how each layer works, the more you can synthesize the totality of who you are to achieve the Divine Adamic blueprint that is your birthright.

Your emotional body provides the "fuel" of loving energy for your thoughts, wishes, hopes and dreams. If you focus on negative things in your life, the lack of health, happiness and abundance, your emotional body will fuel that as well, with sorrow, anger, fear and illness.

The emotional body works in two ways: It takes in information from your surroundings and gives out fuel to your convictions. The basic "intake" function of your emotional body is that of a warning system, an alert radar always ready with a nudge in the proper direction. Remember that your energetic body and all of its layers are in dimensions higher than your physical senses, which are accustomed to sensory input only from 3D.

With that higher placement comes higher sight, from a perspective that your eyes, senses and left brain could not before reach. Learn to sensitize yourself to what your emotions are saying, for they have a ready answer if you acknowledge them and listen carefully. Especially now, in this time of escalating frequency and psychic development, it is imperative that you learn how to control your emotions and not let your emotions control you.

Keeping Your Emotional Body Clear

That which is your emotional body is actually the auric layer closest to your physical self. Your language reflects this "layer of existence" in many clichés: He was beside himself; he let his emotions get the better of him; he let his anger rule him; he was blinded by rage. We say this: Your emotions were never meant to rule you. Your ego was never meant to rule you. These are merely aspects of self that were designed as a protection and warning system. Have you noticed that when you act "against your intuition" you are never happy with the results?

What you call intuition is actually incoming information from your energetic layers. This process will get stronger as you expand into 4D and regain true communication with Spirit in the higher realms. You will develop new levels of mental and emotional control as you find out how truly powerful you are. Remember that detachment and compassion must rule your behavior, as is God's will. Otherwise, you will create chaos around you, and more negative karma as well.

What happens when you lose control of your emotions? Giving in to your emotions . . . does what? It gives you an excuse for not being in control. Most human societies do not teach children how to be in control of the different aspects of their total being. Since you do not view yourselves as "energetic beings," you do not yet know to include the proper teachings to your children. Learning to read, write and do math is not enough to prepare them for life. Teach your children that all life is precious and sacred. Teach them compassion, teach them meditation, teach them humility, teach them that they are so much grander than they know. Teach them to rule over their emotions and not let their emotions rule them. How? Children learn by watching their parents and other adults interact.

The best way to teach your children is by example.

Indeed, the greatest tragedies in your history are incited by emotions ruling over logic, or lack of compassion and too much logic. As Buddha often said, "Choose the middle way." Do you see? That is the path to enlightenment. No extremes, in either direction, should rule your life. You should not be ruled by any one or any thing save for God's will. You are each and every one an expression of God, complete and whole unto yourself. This is an integral part of the free will directive that governs your corner of creation.

You were originally designed for God to directly experience His physical creation from within the earth realm. Your emotional layer translates the wonders of your plane of existence, to enjoy and find happiness in the sunshine, the flowers, the laughter of a little child. And when you feel sad, or there occurs some physical trauma to yourself or loved ones, your emotions are the path through which you grieve and heal.

Even there, your language says, "He wallowed in his grief." What does that mean? That he got "stuck" at that level of emotional process. You become emotionally stagnant when you expend all of your conscious energy into a past that you cannot go back to change or fix. You must travel forward past this point and find compassion through forgiveness to move beyond. Only then can you gather all your energy for the "now."

All of these accomplishments, compassion, forgiveness and a positive perspective, are facets of the emotional body. So are the baser emotions, like anger, greed, lust, envy and vengeance. By baser we mean this literally, for emotions are expressed in an ascending scale of frequency, from lowest to highest. Anger makes you sick? Absolutely. Laughter is healing? Yes, indeed! Anger cuts into the aura as surely as a knife slices through flesh. All low frequency, fear-based emotions damage the aura, causing blockages which lead to disease and aging. The higher emotions, or love-based emotions, actually charge your body with energy and help to quicken healing.

Once you understand how this process works, it will become a simple choice that you make each time you respond rather than react, each time you forgive and move on, each time you hug instead of fight. Ascension requires a total make-over, a change of attitude and a change of behavioral patterns. When you learn to love all human beings, all living things, you will move into Higher Self, and Higher Self will move in with you!

Each layer of the human energetic body is crucial for total change. The emotional body carries much of the load, for it is the fuel of emotion that propels meditation, prayer and faith. You may argue that all of those things are the concern of the spiritual body. Yes, you are right, but you cannot separate the layers into distinct functions. Each contributes to the total energetic being that you are. Please study this sentence for a moment, and determine what it means to you:

A prayer said with heart-filled gladness shoots directly up to Spirit.

Now look at it again, with our higher perspective added: A *prayer* (spiritual layer) *said* (mental and physical layers) *with heart-filled gladness* (emotional layer) *shoots directly up to Spirit.* These are the physical, emotional, mental and spiritual steps through which you will learn to materialize that which you desire—this is the power of Divine Creation you carry inside you!

Your thoughts, wielded by your intent, fueled by the gratitude of total faith, will bring in anything upon which you focus your attention. Each creation begins at a high vibratory level, where thoughts float and form into ideas. As you "solidify" your goal, you draw it down in descending frequency. *You create your own reality through vibratory frequency changes all around you.* Such is the power of a human!

So, keep your emotional body clear and bright. How? Focus on happiness. Seek it not outside yourself but inwardly.

Temper your day with joy, fill your time with fruitful focus and usefulness, and you will be happy. It is far easier to cultivate a positive attitude than a negative one. It takes less energy and is much more rewarding.

Negative attitude is a big stumbling block on the metaphysical path. You must first acknowledge that you have a negative attitude, which is hard. Why? Because then you step into "ego" territory, which is not willing to admit that it/you are doing something wrong. Again, good, bad, right and wrong are all parts of a whole that does not need those parts. Do not judge yourself or others; that mode of thinking carries a negative vibration. It is far better to imagine each person as reaching their highest potential, for that is the kindest perspective you can have for them. Whatever they are doing at the moment may not be in harmony with their greatest good, but that is no longer your issue. Detachment is vital for compassion to abound.

These are one-sentence reminders of facts you have no doubt heard before. And here is another thought: Detachment is release of the personal ego, so that you no longer care about the outcome of a situation. Once you release all personal attachment to what you or anyone else has to gain, that situation no longer has any emotional hold on you. Keep and hold the emotion of gratitude in your heart, and let all the rest go. Yes, ascension can be that simple!

STRESS, YOUR EMOTIONAL BODY, AND YOUR HEALTH

Though many of you are at different levels of metaphysical evolution, please remember that your overall health relies on the restructuring and maintaining of the physical chakra system. As you evolve into your "light body," make sure to keep those first seven energy centers clear and running smoothly, root to crown. The bottom three chakras (below the belt) must be integrated with the upper three: throat, third eye and crown. The fourth, or heart chakra, will act as a fulcrum for the three above and the three below.

Learn to lead with your heart—this is vital advice.

Many of you who are shifting right now have aches, pains and phobias flaring up to be cleared. Know that these old, buried issues arise from the galactic attunement you are all processing in this time of great change. Allow for it to happen naturally and know that all will be resolved as you reawaken and reabsorb all facets of Higher Self. Do not be concerned with the higher levels until you begin to sense and interact with them. Trust that the changes are coming in with Divine Timing, under grace, for each individual.

We humbly remind you here that the Circle of Grace is a wonderful tool to clear and balance the entire human being, at all levels. For the emotional body, the Circle of Grace drains away stress through the energy meridians of the body. It is at once a physical and auric clearing. How could it not be, since the two are so energetically intertwined? The aura feeds and clears itself and its physical core through energy currents that penetrate the skin directly into the nervous system. Your nervous system also helps to anchor the aura into the body and, since stress is processed in the emotional body, the interconnection between the two is vital.

Dear ones, *stress is low-grade pain.* Pain is not an "imaginary" or "invisible" thing. Pain has mass, it has density. Stress has mass and density, too, but both of these forms of pain are invisible to your eyes and to your physical senses. Pain exists in the same dimension as your auric body. Just because you cannot see it doesn't mean it is not there! Your body must deal with pain and stress as physical intrusions that lodge within you, causing pressure that can eventually change your internal structure. When energetic blockages become chronic, they invade your physical core, affecting your health and causing symptoms of illness.

If pain and stress were not real physical things, you would not feel them. Do you wonder, sometimes, when something emotionally painful happens and you stuff it away (you deny its expression), where does it go? It does not go far. It stays magnetized to your field—your electromagnetic field—as a pocket of dense matter in your aura. The more stress you stuff into it, the bigger the pocket gets. The bigger it gets, the closer to the body it grows. The aura shows damage years before a person takes ill. For some of you who carry much auric damage, overcoming illness becomes the goal of your life.

Another reason for learning to govern and clear your emotional body is that is where the stress is (at first) intimately stored, to prevent from overloading your physical nervous system. Pain is magnetically absorbed into the energy of your meridians; as you well know, your nervous system carries signals of pain. It actually carries the pain, too, which must be routinely cleared so that the nervous system can repressurize and rebalance with an intake of new, clear energy as fuel for all levels. That is why regular care and maintenance of the aura is so vital to your overall health. That is also why we have stepped forward now to teach you the Circle of Grace, which is your body's natural clearing process.

Please keep in mind that there are never any "gaps" in this energetic circulatory system. We have spoken of the releasing aspect, moving the pain-filled energy down and out of the nondominant side of the body. In the normal pattern, the dominant (right) side of the body is automatically taking in fresh, clear energy into your meridian system. This new influx pushes ahead of it the old, tainted energy that is released through the (left) hand and foot chakras of the nondominant side. In the blocked patterns, universal energy comes in directly through your crown chakra, replenishing your system from the top down as the clearing takes place.

Remember, there is never any energetic drain without energetic gain.

There is superb perfection in every detail of the Divine Plan, dear ones, and you were superbly designed!

DEFINING THE METAPHYSICAL PATH IN THE NEW MILLENNIUM ENERGY

In this time of accelerating frequency and planetary ascension, many new teachings are percolating up to man's consciousness. Though it is only a small portion of you—as in the example of the hundredth monkey—it only requires a small percentage of believers, or seekers, to affect the whole of the human consciousness. Each and every one of you has the capacity to do so much, so much that you do not yet realize.

The rub here is that, in order for you to believe that you are more than just a body, you must needs experience a few episodes outside of your body for the real truth to sink in: *You Are Eternal!* You are the culmination of all the lives you have ever lived. It has been a long, hard road for you in the 3rd dimension, locked into linear thinking and linear time. But do not despair and do not fear death. In the higher realms, death is rebirth! Once you walk through that portal of death, you, too, will know that death is only an exit door back to your true existence, up to a higher reality. You reunite with Spirit each and every time. We are always there waiting, your guardian angels, to welcome you back and lead you home. You are all brave warriors, angels too, hidden in tiny, heavy bodies with no recollection of your true grandeur.

Know that you volunteered for this "heavy" duty. Know that you all stood in line to be in this, the "last" lifetime on the 3D karmic wheel. In this lifetime, some of you will graduate from this school of planet earth. Many will continue on, without even realizing that a choice was possible and that they could translate into a new reality if they so desired. If this makes no sense to you, then ponder on this: All dimensions inhabit the same space. They are separated by their different octaves of frequency.

You lightworkers know who you are by now, in the dawning of this new millennium. You are the forerunners of change, those that chose faith and a higher frequency of reality. For you, this "coming home" will be quite a party, as we welcome you back with great love for your job well done. Some have already paved the way and translated over, leaving their bodies behind. That, too, is your choice, which Spirit does not judge—the Eternal You is still going home to be greeted by the same celebration!

Can you imagine being able to take your body with you? Learning to translate to a higher dimension happens on all levels that your body inhabits—many dimensions, but mainly the 3rd, 4th, and 5th. The real challenge is teaching the physical body to translate as well. Bringing together all aspects of self, which you term self-realization, is the conduit by which you learn to access Higher Self. The ascension process is a multi-layered plan, as are your bodies, as are our spiritual hierarchies, as are the galaxies, the universes and all the multi-dimensional aspects of the body of God.

All that is, you see, is really All That Is!

In order for you to achieve wholeness, to integrate all of your layers, they must be cleared and balanced. You must be healthy at all levels! Lightworkers, heal and clear each other. Exchange energies and share your knowledge. Prepare together, so that you may work as teams when mass healings become needed. Do your daily meditations, do group work, keep learning and seeking learning.

And yet . . . you must each find your own path in life and learn to walk it. You cannot help others by pushing them forward on their path, or yours, without their consent. The final test is of each of you alone, your consciousness reaching up to meet Higher Self, trying on your light body for size. Through meditation with the Circle of Grace exercise, come to us for alterations on your new "light garment." The work you do now is quiet. The progress you will make is internal, not external. This path is not a journey of the feet, but rather a journey back to your soul, back to True Consciousness, away from the schoolroom that is Mother Earth.

The goal of ascension can only be reached by welcoming in the higher energies around you, above you and below you, and integrating them into your energetic being. How? Through your faith that anything is possible! This mind-set is in direct contradiction with all you have known until now—the separation from Spirit that duality requires. Have you noticed that the further away you stray from God's truth and Mother's needs, the harder is your life? Please, connect back into the earth, hear her gentle voice, feel her powerful, thrumming body under your feet as the true mother to you that she is. Nurture her as she nurtures you all.

How to feed the earth? Studies done by your scientific community have discovered that when an energetic healer is at work, his/her brainwaves and electromagnetic field (aura) blend to match the earth's resonance. You meld into her frequency and thus draw strength from her electromagnetic fields. Do you understand now that you can merge with the mother simply by reaching out with your will, in meditation or even in walking motion? As you can tap into her strength so, too, do you feed her. You feed her with your spiritual energy, your wishes, hopes and dreams. Your negative energy, anger, fear, and doubt, and the pain that you healers pull off of people, is also directed downward to feed the earth's momentum.

Flow down, feed the ground and recycle as positive energy. This is a good healing mantra to use to direct the release of negative energy, each time you lay hands on another or work on yourself. Even the Circle of Grace that humans unconsciously do while asleep, also feeds the earth. She does not distinguish between positive and negative energy; remember, no energy is ever lost, merely transformed to another state. She assimilates the negative energy, uses it as fuel and throws it back into your 3-4D world . . . as weather. Watch the weather, children, take note when it rages; there you will find your own rage, transformed into the cycles of seasons that grow your sustenance.

Do you now see why each and every human's rising awareness is so vital to the planet? For those of you who look at the current state of your global politics and feel helpless to change anything for the better, we say, think again—your energy is vital to the whole planet! You can make a difference! A big difference! From our perspective, we stand in awe to watch the healers amongst you tune into the earth's electromagnetic fields each time you lay on hands. You take on her mantle of grounded energy, which you then pass on to the receiver. Know that you are blessed with Divine Grace each time you do this, each time you circumvent logic, follow the path of your heart and wield the power of the cosmos.

BE THE HEALING ENERGY

As above, so below—you channel Divine energy from above, earth energy from below. Know that this is huge power, wielded by very tiny tools, which always makes us proud to watch you work. In the face of defiance and ridicule, push on, gentle warriors, for you have Spirit on your side. Hold the new frequency, hold up your light, and let it cast its loving spell wherever you choose to stand. Be the healing energy, feel it like a soft shawl that you draw about your shoulders to ward off the chills. Know that this is a cloak of honor that you don each time you reach out in God's name to help another human being on the path to healing.

Your goal, any goal, is established in order to define the journey to it. The true wealth in life lies in the journey. Not in what you amass around you, but what you build within. That is the soul's true treasure, the wisdom that the soul seeks from life to life: The qualities of learning that you gain and the love that you create, you take with you. Naught else but that—the rest is all left behind.

Yet your goal here is assured—no matter what you do or how you do it, God always beams down upon you. *All is as it should be.* You cannot do it wrong, and you will never finish. That is the nature of a classroom, is it not? One with a kind-hearted teacher. And that is the true secret: Put forth your kind heart, and all the rest will follow. Put forth your kind heart with every breath, with every thought, with every motion you make. Your very kindness will protect you against the perceived evil of your world. Again, good and bad are different perspectives on the same whole. If you are thirsty, is not a half-cup of water enough to quench your thirst? If you complain that the glass is only half full, you are missing the gift by a mile. Know that the glass will always be full enough to slake your thirst; that is, simply, faith.

One of the things we find sad in your world is the distorted view of faith. Many people are still locked into specific religions and will not even peek over the box they grew up in. If you would only raise your sight from the dogma that drags you down and separates you from God and look up in order to find God. Faith rises above all religions, teaching to all the same thing: Love, love, love. Do not feel separate from God; to reach Him, merely close your eyes. You carry the Divine Source within, each and every one of you.

Do not let religious fervor blind you from God's presence—that is the saddest of all, the atrocities done in His name. If

you look carefully at the true teachings, they all say the same:
Honor God, honor thyself, thy family and friends. Do not kill.
Do not lie. Do not envy others for what they have. Stay true
to the one God, and He will provide all of your needs. Has He
not done so already, on your beautiful planet called earth?
Look around, and you will see His hand in the perfection of
every detail of life.

So, stand up and take pride in being "a piece of God." Have
you noticed that a prayer sent with devotion and high emotion
is much more effective than the quiet begging and pleading
you were accustomed to in the old energy? Come stand beside
us, metaphysically speaking, and work together with Spirit to
bring in the next evolutionary level of humanity: You lightworkers are now being fitted with "light bodies."

It has been a long and difficult process, for you are the first
humans to change their own physical chemistry through the
process of intent, through a change in perspective. We praise
and marvel at this accomplishment. We wish to help you finish
gracefully, in Divine Timing, and translate up into the next levels of dimensional reality. Then, we will be very proud and
humbled to meet with you directly and shake your hands.

SHIFTING GRACEFULLY
WITH THE MILLENNIUM ENERGY

Welcome to the Aquarian Age, the Age Of Man. Those of
you who chose to stay behind and shine their light for others
are doubly blessed, both for their accomplishments and their
sacrifice. Even that is not quite an appropriate word, for "sacrifice" has a negative connotation. In giving up, you move forward more quickly.

Do you follow?

We hope you will!

Your lessons are coming in hard and fast now. Be kind to
yourselves during this time of fluctuating energy. Rest often to
counteract the heavy weight of ascension. For despite the
heaviness, it is a "pulling up process." The higher the frequency, the shorter and faster the energy waves that thrum through

your bodies. Time is expanding and contracting, changing in its fluidity as it changes its structure. Even the air itself feels heavy on some days, yet on others, everything sparkles and shimmers with an essence of new energy.

This time of "cosmic fitting" is a precious part of the journey. The awakening is always sweet. Again, be kind to yourselves, drink much water, rest often and take heart despite the heavy, depressing energy shifts you are going through. As this process accelerates, there will be moments when you must surrender to it and let us help you. Do this through meditation, through sessions with us, and by resting, napping or running the Circle of Grace through your body when you feel tired.

Follow your body's feelings as a gentle monitoring system. Tired? Rest. Hungry? Eat. Need to stretch? Go walk. Leave behind the music and the headphones. Pay attention to what is around you. See if you can feel the drumbeat of Mother Earth's heart—her pulse is closer to your own than you realize.

You have many books available to help you along the metaphysical path. It is now time to stop reading, children, and start doing the work! We do not mean here for you to stop studying, learning and stretching your awareness. That is the soul's purpose of your human existence. What we mean is that now, as you anchor yourself in 4D, the earth's energy is beginning to support those very gifts that you have been praying for: The expansion of the senses into full sensory perception, and the added vision of inner light.

This will all still happen gradually, to allow you no harm in the process.

There are many amongst you who are awakening, yet are metaphysically unaware. Because they do not understand the rising energy and the sensory gifts that it brings, they will think they have gone insane. Look for them, pick them up off the ground and impart your healing energies on them. They will become, eventually, the devoted zealots who move the cause forward. Once your scientists have embraced your spirituality, they will be far louder than you are! We repeat, humble, humble, humble. Let them broadcast the news as if they had discovered it themselves. Indeed, in their eyes, they will have.

It matters not, as long as you all move forward on the path back to God-Self. Once the human consciousness has been fully awakened, then the floodgates will open and the changes will be quite intense. Stand ready, dear ones, and stand steady, holding up your light to show them the way. Ground yourselves well, so that you are not knocked off balance by the tidal rush of catch-up seekers. Find your bliss and your perfection along the way, for it is truly the journey that counts. The purpose of all of your human journeying is, simply, learning and growing and expanding until you can once again merge with the I Am All That Is.

We know that we will meet you there.

Chapter Three

The Mental Body

In this chapter, we will discuss the use and form of the mental body. It is the third layer of the dense etheric body, after physical and emotional. It separates the emotional body from the spiritual body. That is part of your difficulty and part of your gift. Inherent in your consciousness is the element of choice, the state of free will that separates you neatly from the other planets and dimensions used for teaching and learning lessons.

We will not here go into the history of the fall of man. Though we are spiritual historians, for the purpose of this work we don the mantles of material mechanics and spiritual surgeons. We focus on how the fall of man changed humans, and how we can help you return to wholeness. No doubt you are wondering, how does this affect me?

We say simply that you lost your conscious link to God. You do not feel God's presence as a physical vibration inside of you (while you are awake, due to the Veil of Forgetfulness). You feel a duality instead, and think that you exist separately from God, which leaves you open to doubt that He exists. Most other sentient species do feel God's frequency within them and know for sure that God exists. Therefore, doubt and duality are not part of their lesson plan. For them, to break God's Law is a horrible experience, for they are in direct contact at all times with the conscious energy of All That Is.

To help you survive this breach as you became denser beings, your aspects were layered so that each would buffer those on either side. The emotional body, if in direct contact with the spiritual body, would awaken your consciousness too soon and reforge the link painfully, before you were ready. Having the mental body layered in between the emotional and spiritual layers insured that this did not happen. This arrangement served you through many lives.

Now is the time for you to awaken, to become aware of your total being, and to begin to function in the higher reality where your interdi - mensional body truly resides.

Having the mental body mediate between its adjacent layers is the perfect balance for you to achieve. The mental body was meant to mediate, not to lead. You see, you were designed to respond to stimuli in layers of information. For every situation, the dynamics are absorbed through your physical senses, then processed through your emotional, mental and spiritual layers. Each layer adds in a level of understanding. The emotional body processes lessons and comes up with an emotional, feeling response. The mental body aims for a logical response, and the spiritual aspect inspires soul advancement through each experience.

In other words, you find synchronicity, self-realization, true health and inner peace when all of your aspects are working together in balance. We call this "wholeness," which has been almost impossible for you to achieve, since you have only experienced life through the physical half of your bodies. You must expand your framework of reference in order to become, and live from, the perspective of a total energetic being that has a physical core. Do you see the "higher mind-set" you need to assume?

Dear ones, wholeness is Oneness with all things, including God.

Before you lost your conscious connection to Spirit, your mental body worked in this way: The left brain directed and carried the awareness of the physical body, while the right brain directed and carried the awareness of the auric body. Your mental body was comprised of the two halves of your brain working together equally. In other words, you were consciously linked to your body and to your aura. In the disconnection, only your *conscious connection* to the right brain was lost. Though you only feel your physical half, do not worry—your auric half is still there, dutifully fulfilling its functions. It is the seat of your imagination, your creativity, your faith, as well as the storehouse of your emotions, pain and stress.

What remains in your conscious awareness is only your left brain—that which controls or directs your physical body. In order to reassimilate, or consciously reconnect with your right brain, you must first reprogram your left brain and teach it to be still at times, so that you may stretch and reach for the silent right side. For most of you, this requires a real effort of will because you have lived solely through your left brain for many, many lifetimes.

Now do you see why you developed into "left brained" technological societies? It was all you had to work with. The more technological your societies became, the more rigidly linked into machines you became. This overused the left side of the mental body, forcing it to take the driver's seat in your recent lives.

Do you understand why imagination, creativity and faith are such nebulous things, which you find so difficult to tap into? It is because you do not have clear, conscious access to your interdimensional aspects. Please, treasure your artists and dreamers. They may not function well according to your left brain standards, but they are not as incompetent as you think! They may seem "wifty" and "ungrounded," but in reality they are functioning at a higher level, receiving stimuli from more than just the 3rd dimension. Treasure your children who have imaginary friends and see fairies in the forest. They do see Spirit, until someone blindly convinces them it is impossible.

To those dear nay sayers, we gently ask, do you see the flow of this pattern? It is now circling back to you! As the earth rises in frequency, so does all life on earth. Now that your senses are beginning to flower into full 4D sensory perception, you, too, may soon see departed loved ones hovering near you and hear voices speaking from other dimensions. What will you do then? Deny, or rejoice? *Heaven is a state of consciousness you can achieve while still in body.* Regaining conscious awareness of the right brain is, in fact, reforging that lost link to Spirit.

And how, you ask, do you accomplish this? There is a big leap of faith to be made here, a reawakening and rejoining to your true Self. Your bible says, "To enter the Kingdom of Heaven, be like a child." Be fearless, be open-minded, be aware of every moment, find joy and wonder in all that surrounds you. To children, all time is Now. Learn to live in the Now, as we do, and we will find each other.

How can we help? We can reach you and teach you how to heal through the Circle of Grace. You will learn how to access your right brain and connect consciously with your auric self. Become one with this process, work with us, and you will be working toward ascension.

THE CIRCLE OF GRACE EXERCISE AND THE MENTAL BODY

In the first chapter, we said that the normal Circle of Grace pattern goes up the dominant side of the body, circles around the head and goes back down the other side. When the energy reaches the top of the head, a separate circle begins to pulse around the crown.

That separate Circle of Grace at the crown can now be explained. That stimulation of the crown chakra is reawakening the right brain connection and balancing right brain to left brain. Remember we said that the Circle of Grace helps each layer process pain, then clear and balance? When you enter the Circle, be aware of the separate circular pulsing at the top of your head. For the mental body, this is a vital part of the new human awakening. If you fall asleep at night while doing the Circle of Grace, even better. It will continue through the night, magnified by your awareness and now your new instructions.

The separate Circle of Grace at the crown has another, very practical purpose. It acts as a "circuit breaker" for the rest of the system, so that blockages cannot back up and lodge in the crown chakra. There forms a horizontal line above the ears, as if you were wearing a hat, beyond which blockages cannot rise. That is where the greatest internal pressure of the meridian system occurs. So, most people who start the Circle of Grace follow the fully blocked pattern first, clearing from the head down on both sides. That is also why, dear ones, some of you have strokes that occur at ear level, around the head.

We will remind you, emphatically, that much damage must accumulate before a health threat of that magnitude strikes the body. The judicious and steady use of the Circle of Grace exercise, plus healing sessions with us, your loving guardians, will prevent that damage from accumulating, even if it is a hereditary pattern. *Remember, hereditary patterns only arise when auric illness reaches your physical core.*

What is your biggest challenge at the mental level? Quieting your left brain-dominant mental body in order to awaken your dormant right brain connection. Too much chatter from the mental body monopolizes your daily awareness. Too many mental distractions prevent you from connecting with the earth, feeling in harmony with all life and remembering who you are. Television has you as a captive audience, telling you what to wear, eat, buy, be, like and want.

Do you realize how much power is in those air waves? But—cosmic humor here—you have the ultimate power. Turn the television set off and go for a walk. Read a book in a silent room, which allows you full focus. Meditating in the Circle of Grace flow every day, even for only thirty minutes, will calm you, release your stress and energize you at the same time. And it's non-invasive!

Work with us in session as often as you wish, and we will impart healing to you at all levels. Now we offer this explanation about our work together: In order to quiet the left brain, we ask that you put it in charge of reporting aloud what you feel. Simply, give it this task and no other. You will find yourself floating in the warmth of your new, extended body. It will feel as if your outer skin is expanding to a bigger size. Your mental focus on what is happening inside your body will eventually link you to your entire being, both physical and auric halves, in proper balance. Then you will truly grow into the new expression of man's potential to become an "energetic human."

When you open a healing session with us, bring to us your aches and pains, yes, but also your questions, hopes and dreams. Voice them to us, and we will help bring them in. Bring us the concepts you wish to assimilate, the questions you have regarding your life, your purpose, your progress. Do you see how healing must occur on all levels? Once you lie down, all we ask is that you track the energy flows through your body and express aloud to us what you feel, as you feel it. Your verbal feedback will help guide our hands. If you fell asleep during a session, know that we worked with you at a subconscious level on emotional, mental and spiritual issues. Or, in some cases, we chose sleep for you while working on deep-set physical block-ages that might cause you discomfort if you were awake.

The Circle of Grace works for each layer of the body in a specific way. For the mental body, the left brain is given a rest from its laundry list of mundane tasks. It is a letting go of your temporary duality and its many details. That is why the Circle of Grace relieves stress to the mental body as well. While the left brain is resting within its inner focus, it cannot get in your way, and you can rebuild a rapport with your right brain. This is also when you have the best inner growth, when the emo-tional and spiritual bodies intertwine to nourish each other with loving energy. This is why Circle of Grace sessions with us are vital to your ascension process.

We use the higher frequencies of love through your spiritual layer to revitalize your other layers. We teach your mental body to relinquish total control, and ease it back into its true place of observing and advising your other aspects. We then energize the emotional body, from which is returned the love with the fuel of human emotion behind it. At the end of each session, we "tune up" your aspects to work better together, nudging them gently into a new configuration of energetic awareness. If this sounds like a repeating round robin, well, it is! All of life is based on the circle. It is the basic shape of the flower of life, the basic shape of all life everywhere.

COMMUNICATING WITH YOUR AURA

As you learn that your emotions are actually "things" in your aura with weight and density—just like pain is to the body—it will become easier and easier to stay in the higher octaves of love, rather than stay in the lower aspects of fear and all of its negative effects. One will just feel good, and the other bad. Not that we want to stress a judgment here, but it is your association with feeling good and bad that will identify the quality of what is happening around you at each moment. That is what should guide the actions of your logical mental body.

You call this aspect of your awareness "intuition." It is not tangible guidance, for it does not spring—in English—from your mental body. This information originates from the emotional body in your auric field, which is currently invisible and inaudible to you. *Your emotional layer communicates with you through feelings.* That's why learning to listen to your "intuition" is so important. Learn to rely on the signals from your emotional body to mediate between your mental body and your physical body. If you only follow the guidance of your mental body, without adding a dose of love from the emotional body, your physical action will be cold and precise but devoid of feeling.

Do you see now how all layers are vital to the proper functioning of your whole Be-ing?

We say to you, please learn to lead with your heart. Pass every mental thought through your heart chakra (or visualize your upper chest, with both physical heart and emerging spiritual heart chakras working together, side by side). This new, expanded heart center is the fulcrum from which the lower and upper chakras will achieve a higher balance. In the new heart-based "energetic signature" you are developing, lead with your heart to best balance the flowering of your gifts.

In the beginning of this chapter, we said that the mental body mediates between the emotional and spiritual body layers. Now, above, we said that the emotional body must mediate between the mental and physical bodies so that all of your actions, thoughts and deeds are of a positive, loving nature. Do you see why it is difficult to separate or differentiate between the layers? Though each has a specific function, the health of the body depends on all the layers working together in synchronicity.

The totality of this we call "waking meditation." *Life is a meditation.* Once you learn to balance all aspects, they will come forth in Divine grace, each buffering the one on either side, all working together in harmony. If this sounds complicated, do not worry. All of your aspects have been working without your conscious knowledge of them. Even as you become aware of them, they will continue their functions. They will not suddenly stop and wait until you issue direct commands. They are ongoing, as are all parts of you that form your individual whole.

This thought paradigm also applies to the Circle of Grace. It is the body's natural cleansing process, which occurs while you sleep. Becoming conscious of it means joining your physical body in the process with a new "awareness" perspective. Observe the sensations, and you will become intimate with your own energetic system. You will learn to lie down and clear yourself as the need arises, getting rid of "bad things" that happen, rather than stuffing them away and accumulating emotional stress and baggage. This baggage collects in your aura as so many pockets of stress, linked to specific chakras or areas in lesson.

Remember, thoughts and emotions have physical weight and density in your aura, just as pain lodges as a solid mass in your body. Now that you are becoming more sensitive to the frequency shifting of the planet, you will learn the truth of all of this for yourself, soon enough!

LIVING IN AWARENESS

So, are you beginning to understand the association between these different aspects of your entire being? You are now at a level of more intense learning, having walked the material path, then to find the spiritual path, then to find us, your devoted guides, waiting to welcome you to the higher realms. These new lessons are internal ones, as you become aware of all of your multi-dimensional aspects.

Once you have reached full awareness, you will begin to reconfigure your aspects to suit your sense of comfort. Some of you live more in your mental bodies, some of you live more in your emotional bodies. Some of you, athletes amongst you, identify themselves through the accomplishments and assets of the physical body. The infinite variety of human expression is one of your most wonderful attributes! Your experiences up the human spiral of evolution have taken thousands of years to unfold. In this millennium time, you are on the verge of a totally new level of life experience.

In the historical progress of humanity's evolution, you first had to learn survival, then how to succeed in life until you began to develop a quest for higher purpose. You had to grow into your layers, first physical (survival), then life (emotional and mental), then quest (spiritual). Finally, now that you are ready, comes the potential for full integration of all facets of Self. You are growing into a true energetic being, into your *full Eternal Be-ing* while still in a human body.

And how, you ask, is all of this done? Dear one, we say again, learn to lead with your heart. Whatever thought you have, pass it through your heart before it passes your lips. If it constricts your heart in pain, do not say those words. Choose better words, more appropriate to Higher Self, words that make you feel "light-hearted."

Light of heart, light of mind, light of body, Light of God. That is the progression, and you have progressed well! Now comes the "getting ready" times. Now is the beautiful birth of a new age of man. As you progressed through the centuries, you have worked on different lessons, different aspects of being, different qualities that the soul is learning.

You have withstood many wars and gained many lessons, difficult as they were. They no longer need repeating, for those of you awakened and aware. Unfortunately, not enough of you fit into this mind-set yet. Even on the verge of this new age of man, there is still war, poverty, starvation and disease rampant around your planet. Since it is mostly in third world countries, you do not see it every day, and it is easy to forget or ignore. You do not need to take on their burdens, except for this: *Be aware of all of it.*

Know that a simple daily prayer, just a few moments of visualizing the downtrodden as healthy and joyous, will help to bring in that potential reality. Picture the earth as clean and shining and healthy, spinning through space like a bright blue jewel. Imagine, if all people did this for a moment each day, how quickly your world would change! Know that all men need uplifting. For each of you that becomes aware, a dozen more of you step closer to that same reality. It will, in time, reach its own exponential curve, and then the global changes will come in much faster.

Now is the time to prepare, to learn and grow, to work together. You need to keep moving, now that the energy is cresting. The stronger the energy grows, the more psychic you become. Stay fluid, open and aware as you flower into full sensory perception.

This, children, is reuniting with God. Re-membering. Re-joining. You are not alone in this. The closer you climb to our dimension, the more we will be able to interact with you and help "pull you up" to join us. On some days, the energy will set your teeth on edge, and on other days you will be quiet or bone-tired. The inconsistency is the worst part; you yearn for stability right now, for a surcease from the "heavy" pressure. Please take advantage of the Circle of Grace! Lightworkers, you must clear yourselves first before you can help others. The Circle of Grace will help awaken your senses and align the energies of your body in an exquisite spiritual attunement, if you consciously participate in the process.

MERGING INTO 4D

When we say that you are in 4D, know that 3D expanded into 3-4D in May 2000. We remind you that it is the earth that is changing, and you are along for the ride. Your solar system is changing, your galaxy, and all the other levels beyond. Those people who are unenlightened and unaware will continue to function in 3D.

You lightworkers and seekers are now expanding into 4D, consciously, along with the planet. We await you in 5D, which because of the great shift is also moving upward. If you cannot grasp this concept yet, we remind you of two things: *All Is One, and All changes together.* Also, as you rise through the dimensions, you will realize that 4D includes 3D. 5D includes 3D and 4D. That is why people stuck in 3D will not perceive the next levels of awareness, while you will still see them clearly and interact with them from your expanded view.

In the same way, every healing session with us is an "altered state," where we gently guide you into the higher energies and tune you up slowly to the new frequency. For those of you still stuck on, "How in hell can this be going on if most people aren't even aware of it?" we answer you with this image:

Imagine a neighborhood street. In every house, there is at least one television set. When cable TV becomes available, some people buy it and some people don't. Some people buy satellite dishes and get lots of new TV stations in a different way. In every house, there is at least one television set. What each person chooses to do with their set defines which stations that TV set will receive. Install a cable box, get a hundred new channels on the same set. Install a satellite dish, also get hundreds of new stations from a different source. Choose not to install anything, and all that your TV set will pick up are public stations, a few dozen or so.

Do you see the different levels? *You have the power to choose.* First, though, you have to be aware that there is a choice to be made! That is your absolute first step, which you have accomplished through seeking information, going to seminars and lectures, and reading many texts, fiction, non-fiction, channeled, non-channeled. Choices, you see? So very many, at so many levels. But if you are not aware that these choices even exist, you cannot take that first step up the metaphysical path.

Remember, that step and every subsequent step must be made on all levels. By this we mean, physical, emotional, mental and spiritual. Think of yourself as a blended "PEMS" being, one that can tune into many different frequencies of existence at once. *You see, you are your own TV set!* What enters your mind and guides your life can only expand as far and as fast as your mental framework of reference will allow.

For those of you who have been on the path for years, this work will be a concise review and explanation of metaphysics. For those readers new to the genre, this work may take many readings and rereadings to assimilate fully. All the levels are built in here, from the simple physical level to the complex universal laws level. You may note that the very narrative tone of this work changes as the material becomes more complex.

Then, as in all of life, it will come back to the beginning again, as you begin not only to heal yourself but to heal your entire life, and all lives that came before.

So, welcome to the new energy. Go to the office every day as usual, but heighten your perspective. See the flowers along the road, admire trees along the way, do deep breathing as you wait at the red light. Expand your awareness into each and every moment. Can you do this? Yes, of course you can—you are created in the image of God, who is the ultimate Creator. You, too, have His creator powers. You are so much more powerful than you realize!

This is what you must practice: being aware. Simply, being aware. Be aware of how you speak to people, be aware of how your food tastes, be aware of how the sunshine gleams on your lover's hair. Enjoy every moment, savor each breath you take, see the Divine all around you.

When you go to sleep at night, join us in a Circle dance. Let us help you to advance. Be aware of the blood flowing in your veins, be aware of the pulsing of your heart, focus on your breathing. Let your thoughts slide away and float as a consciousness on the inner sea of your body. The journey upward is inward. The best thing to learn is not to get in your own way! Strive for balance, reach for a kinder tone, be like unto the earth its own heartbeat.

We speak here of merging. The more you merge your awareness into all that is around you, the higher your awareness will take you. Practice first, before you take off and fly. When we speak of All That Is, we speak of God. Do you now understand that perspective? Being aware, every second, is living in the Now. Once you master that, you can begin to affect all that is around you—specifically time—past, present and future.

Back to the circle, children! There are no accidents at this level. What you will see is the emergence of synchronicity. Watch for it, it will happen more and more around you. Once you begin to rely on it, then you will have arrived!

Where? Arrived at true faith.

Put up a bird feeder near to a window where you can watch, for the birds have a vital lesson to teach. They are tiny messengers of Spirit, showing the cycle of abundance that keeps them fed through the seasons of their little lives. When your bird feeder is full, they arrive and sing to their friends that breakfast has been served. If you forget to fill the feeder, they fly by and sing a sweet complaint for their friends to move on. They are tiny and fragile, yet all around them is food. Mother Earth nurtures them and keeps them fed. They survive every day, happily, singing their messages of loving abundance back and forth in the trees above your heads. Have you noticed?

Be like the little birds. Arise each day, and reach for what you know will be there—everything you need. Once you do that, and truly believe it, what you desire will come true. That is living in true faith. The energy within you will rise exponentially from your efforts, and others will feel it.

Go forward, then. Just begin to walk, and do it in strength and vitality, with awareness of your body, your emotions, your thoughts and your faith, all swirling around you in gentle layers of invisible, silken energy. The more you reach for wholeness, the more you feel it, the more quickly it will happen. Once your mental body has fully accepted this perspective and begins to function from this perspective, your entire Be-ing will shift accordingly, from physical 3-4D human to energetic 5D human.

The entire millennium shift and the ascension of man to a light-bodied human happen together when you blend all of your aspects, become reconnected to your total energetic being, and begin to function as Higher Self. In other words, you must catch up physically with all of the spiritual knowledge you have gained thus far. *None of it will work until you start living it, on all levels.* That is how you change your chemistry, through a new, higher perspective of being reconnected to Self and therefore to God.

So, we come back to the beginning, as a circle always does. We said that your challenge had been created by disconnecting your conscious awareness of Spirit, and that you must needs find it again. We explained what this process feels like, and how you can participate in discovering and actively honing your spirituality.

You can also think of this process as living every moment with a love-filled heart. Once you begin, it will become easy, it will feel right; it will feel much better than you have felt in a long time! Use the Circle of Grace to regain and maintain your health, to keep yourself balanced and energized. Use the Circle of Grace in your healing work to find and release blockages, to help others regain their health and balance. Teach them how to be self-healing, how to have mastery over their health, their energy level, and their lives.

Teach them the Circle of Grace.

You will achieve a higher balance. You will regain your connection with Spirit. You have already affected the balance of the New Age, bringing it in with ease and grace. We are very proud of your accomplishments. Your "reaching up" will affect all of the dimensions above you, as any shift affects the whole. Do you see why we are so proud of you? For all of the help that we offer, you are doing the hardest portion of the work.

We are very grateful, and humbled, by the opportunity to serve as your guides.

Chapter Four

The Spiritual Body

I n this chapter, we will endeavor to explain the workings of the spiritual body. It is the fourth layer of the human's dense etheric body, which is comprised of physical, emotional, mental and spiritual aspects. The spiritual layer is set furthest away from the physical core. In between are the emotional and mental bodies. We previously explained that if the spiritual body were layered against the emotional body, it would be impossible for you to maintain the Veil of Forgetfulness. It would be ripped away long before you were ready, causing you pain and harm in the harsh reconnection to Spirit.

We said, in the first chapter, that true healing will come when science and spirituality meet and merge. We also said that true healing will be attainable with the help of three different types of healing practitioners: medical, psychological and energetic.

And now we may add that all of this, the healing and the not healing, is directed by the spiritual body. *The main function of the spiritual body is to learn life lessons, and its programming is the lessons.* These lessons are what you, in your eternal Spirit form, direct to happen in each lifetime. Do you now see what a round robin life really is? As always, layers upon layers, and layered levels of understanding that build on each other.

This is the pattern of how reincarnation works: *Spirit concep - tualizes, the body actualizes, then the soul synthesizes.* You go "into body" to create situations needed to further your soul's evolution toward reunion with Spirit. Here is a simple example: For those of you dealing with addiction, you must stop smoking tobacco while you are in body. If not, that physical addiction continues back to Spirit with you, unresolved. You cannot smoke a cigarette if you do not have a body! The physical addiction must be dealt with "in body," or carried over as a lesson for the next lifetime to face again and finish.

For the purpose of the Circle of Grace work, we Brothers see ourselves as "material mechanics," teachers of how things work in the True Reality of Spirit. We will not elaborate on the whys, wherefores and specific details of philosophy or history. That is why we mention things such as the fall of man and do not offer a long explanation. That you can find easily elsewhere and draw your own conclusions (that is exercising your free will!). We strive here to explain to you how things work energetically, and lead you with grace and ease into a higher frequency of existence.

LEADING WITH YOUR SPIRITUAL BODY

In what you call the Fall of Man, the Veil was drawn down and you lost your conscious link to God. You are still, in all layers of your energetic being, very much linked to Spirit. As you know, your conscious mind operates very differently from your unconscious mind. In the same way, your emotional body processes incoming stimuli and produces an emotional response, while the mental body takes that same stimuli and offers a logical response. Do you see why two people may react so very differently to the same thing? One may constantly lead with their mental body, and the other with their emotional body. Indeed, that is the main difference in perspective between men and women.

The one that leads with the spiritual body, however, stays calm and observant. She/he surveys the situation and absorbs the reactions of the inner layers, physical, emotional and mental. Then the spiritual person speaks, having brought all layers into balance, and says the truth, clear of ego or drama. Those parts have been absorbed and processed, leading to the spiritually correct response, which is directed by the heart.

So learn to respond rather than react. What is the difference? About ten seconds, to process at all levels and then speak clearly. Do you realize that when you react to something, you are matching that vibration? If anger is directed toward you and you react in anger, no good can come of that moment. If you pause, rationalize, emotionalize, then pass it through your heart (metaphysically speaking), your heart will always lead you true and your answer will always be loving.

As you progress through the levels of life lessons, you will gain new understanding and compassion for people as you begin to see where they are "stuck" in their lessons, and why. For those of you talented at seeing life lessons, know there is no greater gift you can give to someone. *Each and every one of you is in body to further soul growth, plain and simple, in order to return and reunite with Spirit.*

The higher your personal vibration rises, the more sensitive you will become to those with discordant energy. You will feel it instantly, not with your everyday senses, but with your whole aura. (Here we refer to the dense etheric body, the four innermost layers of your total energetic being.) Your aura is normally three to six feet all around you, depending on whether it is expanded or contracted. It also stretches above and below you, creating an oval sphere of electromagnetic energy that is truly your "outer skin." If you stretch out your arms, you will transverse the diameter of your dense etheric body. When someone approaches, your two auras meet at six feet apart from your physical cores. That is when you begin to "read a person" and formulate how well your frequency matches theirs.

Do you realize that "first impressions" come from your aura? From your spiritual layer! When you get "goose bumps," as you call it, what happens? An uncomfortable feeling slides over your skin (incompatible frequency) that raises your hairs on end (outer physical response) and then your gut tightens (inner physical response). Do you see the direction of this warning feeling? It flows from the outside in. It flows from your spiritual layer, through your logic and your emotion, then into your body as a physical warning that something approaching is not compatible or is not in harmony with your greatest good. On the other hand, you will also feel when a person with a very compatible frequency approaches you! First impressions actually occur before you get close enough to shake hands.

Back in the days when you were scraping for survival and hiding from larger beasts, your "auric radar" was a very vital part of your consciousness—it saved your life many a time. Now, as you grow more civilized and approach a new level of evolution, you are becoming sensitized to new levels of reality, of information, of sensation. You are beginning to feel and communicate with your aura and, thus, with Spirit!

BLENDING SPIRITUALITY WITH RELIGION

Please remember that no energy is ever wasted. All is recorded by the spiritual body, both the incoming data and the backlash of the individual's physical, emotional and mental reaction to the stimulus or situation. That is how the soul learns and grows. That is how your akashic records are compiled. With all of this new information flowing in from Spirit, many of you are struggling to make it reconcile with your prior beliefs about God and faith.

Part of the problem you now have with established religions is the "blind faith" aspect that lingers from fear-based patterns of earlier times. You were required to believe whatever religious pattern you were born into, and there was usually grave punishment for those who did not. Now you are reaching for new, higher truths, and find your feet entangled in the old ways. Keep the best of what you like and kick the rest away! Faith is an internal quest, never beholden to another man. Those old traditions also contradict the "free will zone" that sets you apart from all other sentient species in lesson.

You were meant to decide for yourself whether or not to believe in God and choose for yourself how to express that belief.

How does each life, and its lessons learned (or not learned), culminate in who you are today? All of your lifetimes of experience are recorded by your spiritual layer. When you "wrestle" with your lessons, you are actually trying to bring your emotional and mental aspects into balance, a balance dictated by your spiritual layer. How is this done? Through your intent! We find it humorous that your scientists have puzzled out about 10 percent of your DNA patterns and have labeled the other 90 percent "junk DNA." Not junk, dear ones, but your own personal akashic records, chock-full of vital wisdom and talents stored at the cellular level that make you who you are today. You carry your own spiritual blueprint within every cell of your body. One day you will access this information and truly understand who you are and the way things really work.

A HIGHER PERSPECTIVE

Many sources have given good counsel and direction as to how to become more spiritual, how to identify and learn your lessons in order to move forward, how to achieve clarity, balance and self-realization. We only seek to explain how things work in energetic terms. Now that you know of the role that your spiritual layer plays in your life, you will begin to understand why you have not had conscious contact with your spiritual aspect or with the other higher aspects of your total being. Here, we will endeavor to show you the difference between human and spiritual perspectives.

To you, the earth is a huge, vast space, almost too big to comprehend. To us, you have been in a narrow corridor of heavy density and linear time. You are "in lesson." You are in the duality matrix. You are in ongoing levels of study, working on different issues throughout each lifetime.

To you, a lifetime is rather long. Modern science has extended life expectancy, as well. Not near to your full potential, not yet. But still, a vast improvement on the first millennium. To us, the passage of a human life is very quick, a morsel of your true existence. It saddens us how you worry so about death, but that is part of the setup, is it not?

You see death as a painful drama, with mourning and weeping. We say, do so if you must, and cry your fill with gusto. To get past those tears, you must shed them. Then move on, for you are still amongst the living. Take comfort that you will see your loved ones again, soon.

Know that on our side there is a glorious reunion for your loved one, a party for the homecoming soul. There is no judgment, but a private life review that only he or she observes. Each person decides how well they did and chooses which unfinished lessons to carry over into the next life.

In the meantime, they have much to do when they return home to the higher realms. In Spirit, we (and you) lead busy, active lives, full of purposeful activities. We have families here, too, often comprised of souls who did their best to "push your buttons" down on earth. That, dear hearts, is being in lesson. When you reunite in the True Reality of Spirit, you thank each other for jobs well done and lessons learned together. Often, the most bitter enemies in human form are tight brothers in eternal form!

This information is offered in the hopes of expanding your understanding of the higher realms. Now that you are beginning to realize that your inner world leads to the higher worlds, it should give you more impetus to meditate. Especially now, when the energy changes all around you are increasing. The planetary frequency is rising, and more and more Divine Light is coming to earth. We in the higher planes are getting ready to welcome you! You will feel us more and more, as time increases the exponential currents of change.

THE CIRCLE OF GRACE EXERCISE
AND THE SPIRITUAL BODY

The changing energy is all around you, inside you, above and below you. Pay attention, children, to Mother Earth as she rises up towards her own ascension. Your spiritual aspect is now being energized and awakened, and will be greatly aided by using the Circle of Grace. Yes, back to our clearing process, and how it helps your spiritual body.

While balancing all of your other aspects, physical, mental and emotional, the Circle of Grace activates your slumbering spiritual gifts and awakens your dormant connection to Spirit. We admit to being impatient for you to achieve this, for you are getting close! The energy right now is frenetic, jagged, too fast, too slow, no time, no rest and no consistency. Carve out a few moments each day; a half hour is good to start with. Lie down and slip into the circle of energy that animates your body! For those of you lucky to have more time, an hour-long session is plenty. For those of you with no time, start the Circle of Grace as you're going to sleep and know that it will continue clearing you through the night, until you awaken.

You will feel an easing of stress, a sharpening of the senses, a rise in synchronicity in your life. Now that you know how it all works, whatever happens around you, pause and seek the lesson. Ask yourself, why did that happen? Why did the universe see fit to remove this from me? To inflict this on me? To destroy this thing I cherished, or steal this tender life I loved. Why? It is all part of your lessons.

You will all reunite in the True Reality of Spirit, soon enough. No energy is ever wasted or terminated; life is merely transformed. In the case of the earth plane, you translate in and out by inhabiting a physical body, entering at birth and exiting at death. Before you are born, we bid you a fond farewell, and wish you Godspeed through your lessons (chuckle). We eagerly await your return, which is far more joyous a process than you realize. It is the birth that is hard, the coming down of the Veil, the separation from you that we in Spirit find so difficult to bear.

Death, on the other hand, is your triumphant return home! That is all it is, merely an exit. A release. A respite. A relief. A transmutation of your life force. You never lose consciousness. You switch over to your full auric self by pulling your energetic body out of its physical shell. *Dear ones, whether you come home with or without that body, you return equally triumphant!*

THE VEIL OF FORGETFULNESS
AND YOUR SPIRITUAL BODY

At the soul level, you agreed to certain built-in safeguards to the Veil of Forgetfulness, which have kept you locked in the duality matrix of 3D. First, there is a "hard-wired" connection between Spirit and the body it inhabits: You are designed to be terrified of losing your body, letting go of it or leaving it, so it may be difficult at first to assimilate these new higher concepts that we offer. Actually climbing in and out of your body might seem ridiculous to you, but you've done it many times, at birth and death and in between.

Second, the overriding rule is: No conscious connection to Spirit. That is how the Veil functions in 3D. Behind it...are we, in the True Reality. You are on the other side, blind to our presence in the upper dimensions, though we see you clearly. In order for this intricate tapestry of karmic reincarnation to unfold, you have been kept unaware, until recently, of the higher realms and of your potential to "be in this world but not of it."

Up until now, the Veil of Forgetfulness has functioned as a separation mechanism that supports the parameters of your free will zone. As a 3D human, you do not know or need to know who your real Spirit self is,who your real Spirit family is. You do not know what lies on the other side of death, nor can you know of the work your Higher Self does while your body and conscious mind are asleep. Many of you still do not know for sure if God exists, for that is the goal you must achieve on your own—free will—your choice. Do you see how the Veil affects and directs your life? It has kept the 3rd dimension in place, separating what you know from who we (and you) really are in the True Reality of Spirit.

There are many among you who do not know that they do Spirit work at night. They can move their consciousness fully into their auras, or astral selves. They can exit the body and move freely in the upper realms, while the body and conscious mind are asleep. You may have no waking recollection of having been out of body, because of the Veil. But for those of you who have flying dreams or falling dreams, you were either out or returning!

Why do you think that nobody really knows what happens to you after you die? The Veil of Forgetfulness, at work. The limitations of 3D require that you cannot remember any part of Spirit life, none of it. Again, this would only confuse you and pull your focus away from the here and now. Though most of these old "reality parameters" are changing with your expansion into 4D, focusing on the Now is one aspect that you are familiar with—you are used to being blind to all but your present moment in time. As you rise into awareness of being in 4D, the Veil will get thinner, allowing your senses to pick up information that was previously beyond your reach. In order to avoid the confusion of "sensory overload," we ask you to consciously focus on your present moment and to be present in every moment!

For that is the best way to get through your life: Focus on the here and now. Focusing on the past is a waste of energy, pure and simple. The ingredients needed to sever past ties? Compassion and forgiveness—for all those concerned (including yourself!), and for all that has happened to you. Both have molded you into the particular consciousness that you are today.

Remember, no energy is ever wasted. All of this information is encoded in your DNA, your personal list of past lives. All that you were, all that you did, all that you learned, all the different ways in which you died. Cellular memory is an intrinsic part of the ascension process. Your own ancient knowledge will surface when you begin to communicate with your higher aspects.

To the beginning student, this might all seem a bit unwieldy. To the devoted seeker, a recapitulation of what you already know. Even if there is only one new idea, one word, one thought of ours that you walk away with, that is good. You will find that each time you reread this text, new information will come forward that you need at that time.

So, if this is all just a big game, you're probably thinking, well, if I don't really die then I can commit suicide and just go Home, right? Sorry, no. There is no escape clause in the human contract. That is, for most cases. Yet, if it is part of the lesson plan, and the family has contracted to study the waste of human life, to generate love in the face of adversity, to learn to hold all life sacred, then that suicide has purpose and will happen. For those who choose to end their lives rather than work out their lessons, their "aborted" lives are sad, for they must be repeated and the same choice faced again.

ADJUSTING TO THE NEW
FREQUENCIES OF ENERGY

Right now for you on earth, time is compressing due to the influx of new frequencies. As the energy rises and becomes palpable, so will your auras! Once you start to feel the presence of your etheric layers, you will require a new "comfort zone," a new, higher balance that is heart-centered. Anything that goes against your heart will become painful. You will begin to feel, at the physical level, those damaged parts of your aura that need clearing. Since the source of all damage is stress, you must release those things in your life that cause you stress at all levels.

The problems you have not faced, you cannot begin to solve. These problems will come right back in your face, time and again. Especially now, as time shortens, the lessons are getting more drastic. Pay attention, define the lessons, walk through them and leave them behind!

The rising energy will allow no less. It can be so frenetic at times that you cannot even focus to meditate as you used to. Do not despair, and do not give up. Simply lie down and do the Circle of Grace. Again, the way up is within. What better way to get there? Float on the cadence of your heartbeat, match your breath to the earth's pulse, and call up your healing circle of universal energy to clear, cleanse and energize your body at all levels.

Know that time will eventually stabilize into a new, circular configuration. You will be able to work with it, around it, and through it. Time is only another aspect of energy. It is the aspect that measures the continuous changing of energy. To us, True Reality is constantly changing, so we see time as variable. That is why we have the freedom to live in the Now. You will, in time (chuckle), grow to understand that perspective.

Many of you are impatient to move forward into the new

energy. We, as your concerned guides, ask you to gain your balance and learn to stand and walk before you start running! Some people wake up one day and declare, "I've decided to devote my life to holistic practices." Then they panic, because they've never even entertained the idea before! These are the newly awakened, the wave after the millennium. You of the wave before, who have bravely volunteered to stay, will find them strewn on your path like so many lost lambs. Most of them will be young adults in their twenties, newly disillusioned by life from the adult view. Take them under your wing and show them how much more there really is to life on planet earth.

Then there are the new children. Watch for the Blues, now called Indigo. You have labeled them as ADD/ADHD—dysfunctional children, needing medication and remediation. In truth, these children are prodigies! They come in with all the spiritual tools you aspire to—living in the Now, self-worth, multi-tasking, experiential thinking and visualization far beyond what you can do today. They can conceptualize something into existence by creating it mentally, then simply make the finished product. These children with "Attention Deficit Disorder" are the first rank of spiritually advanced humans to be born on this planet in all of your recorded history!

Find every receptive teacher that you can and explain to them this higher class of kids. Give them the right tools to handle these new children, and theirs will be a glorious teaching experience. Nurture these children, be kind to them but do not patronize them. Treat them with respect, and they will respect you back. These are little adults, with a far higher perspective than you were born with. *For them, the Veil is thinner.*

Teach them that there is value in everything they do. Teach them to meditate, to be still, and to rest there a while. Teach them the Circle of Grace!

BRIDGING THE DIMENSIONS

Now, you may ask, what comes after the spiritual layer? The aspects become much thinner, you could say diaphanous, because of the higher frequencies that place your outer layers

in 5D and above. The form and function of your entire energetic Be-ing is beyond the scope of this text, but we will say
that you are much, much larger than you know! There are
inner aspects of you tied deep into the planet, and outer
aspects of you that reach out into space past your globe.

There is a very, very distant aspect of you, *all of you,* as a
totality of human consciousness that surrounds your planet. It
reaches out to the universe in an "energetic signature" that
speaks of humanity to other races in the multitude of universes
that comprise the collective body of God. Oh, yes, that signature is becoming apparent to the higher realms as the incoming Divine Light strengthens and adds power to your distinc-
tive human energetic imprint. One could say that you have
made the first step toward becoming a global presence to
other global presences around you.

Do you follow?

We hope you will!

There is still much work to do. We are glad to say that the
momentum is increasing, as are the many new experiences you
are having in the 4th dimension. That is where you are now, in
the psychic corridor between the 3rd and 5th dimensions.
There is beginning in many of you a flowering of the senses,
opening up to new stimuli with a hazy frequency, still distorted
as the channel is not fully tuned in yet. With the exponential
curve of time, this awakening will become more widespread,
and "miracles" will become more abundant in your news.

Why will some come into awareness, and others not?
Remember, all dimensions occupy the same space, yet exist as
separate bands of frequency. 3D is included in 4D. 3D and 4D
are both included in 5D. From where we sit we can see all these
levels, and more. From where you sit, you can only see the levels that you are "keyed" into. Once you are fully anchored in
4D, you will still see and interact with people in 3D. Those in
3D, however, cannot see past their own frequency range—they
will remain unaware of 4D until their senses also expand.

The closer you get to matching your energy to the higher
levels, the closer you will get there physically. When you work
with us in healing sessions, bring us this concept, and any oth-

ers that require help to assimilate. Growth in understanding is crucial to heal and meld each layer of your energetic body. *Please, see yourself as an energetic being with a temporary physical core!* Then your comprehension of metaphysics will leap forward quickly.

Once you learn the function and balance of each of your aspects, you will ease your way into a new, higher reality. When your mental body understands its place and role, then new talents will be within your reach. Once you learn how to combine the emotional body with its driving fuel of feelings, to the spiritual body with its pure faith, you will be strong enough to heal, to manifest instantly and to become consciously interdimensional.

So, what is the true role of the mental body? It creates the thought form for the prayer (spiritual layer) that is fueled by feelings (emotional layer). Then the mental layer must get out of the way! You are so used to leading with logic that you discount the power of faith plus feeling. You have no idea of your true power!

We ask those of you doubters who insist on physical proof for everything, how do you then explain your faith? If you say, "Oh, that's different," then we will gently disagree. It is the same. It is the other side of the same coin. It is science and spirituality, physics and metaphysics. The answer lies in learning both sides, then learning to merge them. It will take mutual acceptance, plus integration of science and spirituality, to find the real truth and real proof that God exists. That proof is in your very cells, as patterns of sentient, energetic holograms waiting to be discovered and deciphered.

Once you begin to physically merge all that you've learned with All That Is, you will find us waiting to help finish your assimilation of the new energies, leading to a higher realm of existence on earth. Keep in mind that Heaven is not a physical place but rather a state of consciousness. Your spiritual progress will lead you to a new life in 5D, where you will, indeed, create Heaven on earth.

As your loving guides, we wait impatiently for our reunion with you, in the True Reality of Spirit!

A Poem for
The Brotherhood of Light

I ask the Brothers, work with me.

I ask for health and clarity.

I will my light to shine clear bright,

All day long and through the night.

I ask that Spirit walk with me,

From Now through all Eternity.

Sara

11/16/2001

Chapter Five

What to Ask Us for in Healing Sessions

I n this chapter, we move on to discuss what is a healing session with the Brothers, and what to ask for. Know that you could be in need of much clearing, but we cannot help you without being asked to step in. Here we stride onto the turf of permission—that which defines the free will zone.

The overriding rule of your lives, which Spirit has always upheld, is that of non-interference. You are in charge of your lives, you see, which we have endeavored to explain. Whether you know it or not, you constantly create your reality as you move forward in time (another thing that will soon change!). Your present reality reflects what you have created in the past. What you are currently creating now will become your future reality.

Is it not better to be consciously in charge? To know you're in charge? To know that you are already a master navigator? We are merely explaining the road rules that exist in the bands of reality which you are aiming to enter. *So, we can only do what you ask of us.* There is a ceiling to this as well, a line drawn which we must obey—*We are sworn never to harm, only to heal.* If you ask something of us during a healing session that we see will bring you harm, at any level, we will not oblige. We will wait with you, work on other things, and keep you in the energy of 5D until your session is over.

We ask that you follow the list of questions we offer in the order they are presented, for they represent layers of healing that are like stairs up a staircase—the most graceful way to climb those stairs is one step at a time. We also recommend that you ask for only one or two things in the beginning. It may take time to get through the accumulated layers of blockage that most people carry from this life and prior lives, as well.

All is coming up to be healed; it must be total, you see, the clearing and balancing of all the energetic layers of each human being—that is what "striving for wholeness" is all about. Whatever clearing and balancing you ask for, make sure that you include the phrase, "at all levels."

The Circle of Grace works to heal you at all levels of your Be-ing.

Also ask for changes to come in gently, in Divine Timing, under grace (chuckle). Remember to wear loose clothing, or at least loosen belts, bras and shoes if you can. **Speak out loud** to us in session, beginning with the Healing Prayer (see end of this chapter and Chapter One) that gives us your permission to connect 4D to 5D. Tell us how much time you have and what you would like to focus on. Once you lie down, hands and feet uncrossed, **lower jaw slack**, please continue to verbalize what you feel as the session unfolds.

You may say, "Left arm releasing." Then a few moments later, you may feel the meridians switch and say, "Left leg now releasing." Whatever crosses your mind or moves in your body, say it out loud. If there is indeed a heavy meridian clearing one day that is uncomfortable for you, merely tell us, "Please tone it down, it hurts here." Or if you feel a blockage, say, "Stuck above the left knee, please move it down and out."

Stay relaxed with deep breathing, and let the Circle of Grace sensations reveal to you what your body is doing. It is a wondrous awakening to an inner reality that you were simply not aware existed. Once you become adept at doing this exercise, your body will automatically begin to release every time you sit or lie down to rest, nap, read or watch TV. When you feel the Circle of Grace begin, thank your body for the clearing and continue doing what you wish, while attaching a parcel of your awareness to the self-healing process moving though you.

WHAT "CLEAR AND BALANCE" MEANS IN HEALING

You will note that each request on the list of questions is phrased to specifically require that each area be cleared and then balanced. Cleared of what? Balanced to what? The first answer is simple—cleared of pain, stress and blockages. For the second question, however, we could write an entire tome, dear ones, in answer. Briefly, we will summarize for you one of the universal laws—that of balance.

All forms of life vibrate in balance, to fit into their environmental niche. When a life form loses its balance, we do not mean that it tripped and fell (chuckle), though in a literal sense, it means exactly that: The life form has stepped out of balance with its environment, and therefore is open to damage until it can regain its balance of health within its environment.

Why do we stress balance within the environment? Because it is the requirements of the environment that dictate the proper frequency vibration for that life form to exist. By this we mean, you are made of earth elements. The earth is changing into a new energetic configuration; you must, by being present in body, change also. Your environment is dictating a change in your vibratory form, and your body is adjusting as best it can. Your awareness can greatly increase your momentum, even guide your metaphysical aim higher.

Do you follow?

We hope you will.

REPOLARIZATION OF YOUR ENERGY FIELD

In this section, know simply this: For life to exist, the Universal Law of Balance requires that energy move away and back to a center point. For you in body, each action is actually two, like motion and rest, breathing in, breathing out. Birth and death. Day and night. Awake, asleep. Depolarized, repolarized. Do you see the ebb and flow of all things? Or, you could say that there is an ebb and flow built into all things in God's creation.

In your awake creator state, you spend the day in various pursuits. Each act you perform causes a depolarization of your

energy—you expend energy to create. Then you must rest and
rebuild your energy for the next day—in sleep, your body repo-
larizes itself. Built into the Circle of Grace is, of course, an
aspect of repolarization that renews and replenishes the polarity of your body, of each system, of each organ, of each cell,
indeed, through simple magnetics.

**So ask us, when you begin a healing session, to repolar -
ize your body at all levels.** Make that a standard request, and
all the work will proceed more smoothly. You will also have
more energy available to you after a session is done, if you
include repolarizing. Remember—we can only do as you ask,
and no more. In this chapter, we offer you for the first time a
primer on how to get ready for where you want to go, for
whom you wish to become, a blueprint for your trip Home.
Happiness comes from within you, not from outside your
being. As you heal, you clear out low-frequency damage to
make room for higher-frequency emotions.

That is why we say, *Find God within.*

Find your joy on the journey, dear ones, and allow us to
guide you gently Home.

CLEAR AND BALANCE MERIDIANS AND CHAKRAS

We advise you to ask for this work first: Please clear and
balance my energetic meridians, then clear and balance my
energy centers (chakras). This is a crucial two-part first step,
clearing first the meridians, then the chakras. Why? They are
roads and crossroads which are all linked. Your pathways of
universal energy must be cleared first, so that we can then
reach the inner organs of your auric system, the chakras, to
begin clearing them.

One leads to the other, you see, and your chakras will actively begin clearing as soon as the meridians can handle the added
load. That is why we say this is a two-part first step towards
clearing and balancing your entire energetic system. That is
also why, you will soon see, that auric and physical damage are
inextricably intertwined, as is the healing of that damage.

So, healing must occur on all levels. Even before reaching

the level of physical illness, auric damage can affect your entire life. You may be in great need of grounding, for example, yet find yourself unable to ground. No matter what you try, nothing seems to work. Why?

You cannot ground yourself if your lower three chakras are energetically blocked or clogged. They must be cleared first, and be in good working order for you to anchor yourself with "grounding cords" from the bottom three chakras and from the sole chakras of both feet. Yes, five cords will ground you well and serve to move you forward because the number five is that of change, of forward motion (1) on a double foundation (4). See it as an easy glide forward, and you will truly gain momentum.

When we begin clearing the chakras you will feel us work with physical heat at the root chakra, spreading up the body to clear each energy center in ascending order. But remember that it may take weeks, or months, to effect a total clearing. It all depends on how much baggage you have "stuffed away" over the years, instead of processing. It also depends on how often you do the Circle of Grace, and your level of focus during the exercise. Your greatest tools are these: Your intent to heal yourself, your willingness to forgive all, and your desire to release your unwanted baggage. The more you do this work, the faster will be your upward progress.

Remember, we exist in the Now and are available as often as you invite us to work with you. Calling us in with the Healing Prayer and then doing a passive meditation will not prove as fruitful as actively engaging in the Circle of Grace, whether by simple intent, mental focus or with the Golden Cloud visualization (explained in Chapter One). Your focus on the work and on your breathing greatly augments the effectiveness of what we do together. This level of focused awareness is also your validation of inner Spirit, for you cannot doubt what you clearly feel and experience!

Here is an important thought to assimilate: At the physical level, the ascension process begins with the clearing and balancing of the lower three chakras, which humanity has lived through for thousands of years. You are leaving behind your "below the belt" existence, based on root (survival), second (family) and third (social) chakras. The challenge of ascension is the conscious opening of the four chakras above the belt (heart, throat, third eye and crown) and integrating them with those below to create a new, full-sensoried, heart-centered "blended Be-ing." *You are ascending, you see, into the fullness of your energetic potential.* Yes, there are many other layers of chakras waiting to be discovered and integrated (especially the new spiritual heart chakra now coming in, explained in the next sub-section), but working on the full seven physical chakras is your first priority, and your very necessary first step.

So, ask us to clear and balance the lower three chakras. Then ask us to clear and balance the four above, and integrate them with the lower three so that all seven work in synchronous harmony. For many people, this part of the process can take months.

You may find yourself crying in session after session, until all your pent-up tears are processed and peeled away. Or you may find yourself in expanding levels of Circle of Grace sessions, as the clearing takes hold and new energy can finally enter your body and flow through, as it was meant to do. After the chakras are individually cleared and balanced, we realign them into pairs, then work on harmonizing the entire system to establish a higher level of function. If you have a physical illness, injury or trauma, we begin the Circle of Grace flow in the reverse blockage pattern, clearing the damage directly to the nearest exit point at hand or foot. Once that has been released, you will feel the Circle resume from the head down both sides (fully blocked and alternating blocked patterns), as the nervous system clears and repressurizes. Eventually, you will shift into the normal pattern, with an influx of new energy coming up the dominant side, around the head, and down and out the nondominant side. The Circle of Grace tends to all ills of your entire Be-ing, children, no matter what the cause of the damage may be. By putting your awareness, your attention, then your intention into the session, you quicken the process and learn to control your body's healing!

Another aspect of clearing and balancing chakras that is important to mention is that they work in pairs. They are mated together, if you will, function together and sicken together. Doctors have noticed that patients with certain types of brain tumors often have rectal tumors; they don't know why but know to test for it. We say here, it is because the first and seventh chakras are paired—root and crown. When one falls out of balance, the other works twice as hard to compensate. If balance is not achieved, both areas eventually succumb to illness. The second and fifth chakras are also paired—abdomen and throat. Finally, third and fourth—solar plexus and heart— work together. The sixth chakra, your third eye, works in conjunction with the other six.

So, if you have abdominal issues, which indicate an energetic blockage in second chakra, plan to spend part of each session with us working on your throat! For each chakra to heal itself, its mate must also be cleared and balanced. Once you add this "double focus" to your energetic healing work, lightworkers, you will see remarkable results. Heal the pairs!

Please do not feel overwhelmed by the more complex levels of the Circle of Grace. Focus on the simple steps we offer first and allow for your understanding to grow apace with your knowledge and experiences. Know that we will lead each of you gently, in Divine Timing, through your transition.

Remember, once your meridians and chakras are cleared and balanced, you can carry illness and not feel ill. In other words, you can still carry the symptoms of that illness and lead a normal life and, as you heal, those symptoms lose their hold and wither away. Indeed, ask anyone who has conquered a life-threatening illness how they did it and they will say, "I didn't accept or believe that I had to die, just because someone told me so." Mind over matter? Yes, indeed. Try expanding that mind, and you will find that you have total control over all matter!

So, once you have a clear, strong, free-flowing Circle of Grace, what to ask for?

CLEARING AND BALANCING THE HEART CHAKRA

Here, we say this to you in warning: If you feel symptoms of physical heart trouble such as dizziness, shortness of breath, nausea, cramping and/or pain in your chest and left arm, make

sure that you are cleared by a physical doctor. These are signs
of heart illness manifesting at the physical level. Remember
that the Circle of Grace does not interfere with any medical
treatment or regimen; if you have physical heart damage, you
need to seek the help of a medical doctor. You can continue to
do the clearing work with us while your physical symptoms are
being treated.

    If the doctor finds nothing wrong, that is good, meaning
that the auric blockage has not yet invaded your physical core.
Yet the pressure/pain that you feel is the presence of a true
physical blockage, at a different level of your being—the energetic level. Symptoms of etheric heart blockage are quite distinct, and often manifest beyond the physical heart area.
When the heart chakra becomes overloaded, the aura spreads
heart blockage across the chest in order to balance out the
pressure in the body. It wraps itself around the torso and
makes itself known as a sharp point under the right and/or left
arm about a hand-width below the armpit. It may also feel like
someone is standing behind you and pushing their thumb into
your right and/or left shoulder blade. One or both of these
specific sensations can also begin on one side, as well, before
manifesting on both sides.

    Heart pressure and blockage can travel across the chest and
wrap around behind you, because for every front expression of
a chakra there is a mate to it in the back. Right now, global
humanity is clearing heart, and you are all reflecting this.
Everyone on the planet is clearing heart [channeled December
2001]. The heartache you are feeling can be released through
the Circle of Grace. Once that blockage is cleared, there will
be no need for you to become ill. We ask you to put aside the
fear of following genetic family patterns—if you can clear heart
before you become ill, there is no need to worry about dying
young, even if it is a family trait. *Please know that it is your mental
and emotional states that create and control illness, not your body.* This
will be fully explained in Section Two, The Universal Laws.

    Do you follow?
    We hope you will.

In order for heart to become the new fulcrum of the human energetic system and the new foundation of the "three above and three below," the power and range of the human heart must expand. There is also another aspect of heart evolving at this time: the installation of a new chakra—Spiritual Heart, also called the Christ Chakra or the High Heart. As this energetic enhancement takes root, physical heart must be cleared and balanced, then paired and tuned to Spiritual Heart. Do you see, dear ones, why this step is so important? It is also one of the largest chakra areas to be cleared and may require several weeks of draining and retuning.

By this we mean, work with us every day or every other day when you are clearing heart. If you wait any longer between sessions, you might feel your heart chakra trying to release on its own. This will cause cramping in the chest and pain down the left arm as energy pockets clog up the path of release. It is at this point that we say—do not be afraid that you are having a heart attack. Simply know that this step must be loyally done. Work with us as often as you can until your physical heart chakra is clear.

You will know your progress, you see, as you become more and more "light-hearted" and there comes into your heart the room for joy to lodge there, instead of sadness. *Love and fear cannot co-exist in the same space, for they have different vibratory fre - quencies that the body cannot hold simultaneously.* This is what you will be manifesting at all levels—clearing out fear and replacing it with love. This means clearing out all low-frequency illness pockets from your being, which allows your total, healed self to vibrate at a higher frequency level. This is what healing means, at the cellular level. This is what ascension is, dear ones, at the cellular level. This is re-joining God's vibration.

As always, layers of meaning, layers of intent and layers of work to be done. Clearing heart can be greatly facilitated by an energetic healer; please do not forget that you lightworkers must work on each other. You are in training, clearing first so that you may help others when the full energy of the Now becomes your new reality. So, work with us and work on each other. Once you are done clearing physical heart, ask for your Spiritual Heart chakra to be fully installed, cleared and balanced to run alongside of your physical heart chakra.

This new energy center began coming in for all humanity at the Millennium, though many of you enlightened ones received it earlier. For most people, it came in around the events of September 11, 2001. This new chakra will expand your heart center to flow across the chest and become the broad-based fulcrum of your new light-bodied energetic system. You see, you must now balance the three chakras below the heart to the three chakras above, with heart in the middle of your ascended energetic form, to bring in your light body. We keep repeating in this text, "Lead from the heart, pass everything through your heart, focus on what your heart says to you." *These are all aspects of working from the heart at the 5D level.*

The energy you are leaving behind is fear-based. Your entire society is based on, and has been living through, the bottom three chakras: survival (money), family (sex) and society (power). Yes, money, sex and power motivate most of your politics, big businesses, news media and advertising. Did you ever stop to wonder why it is all so negative? Because none of the "base chakras" have been heart-centered or heart-influenced. As you move into the higher energies, you must understand that we work in a love-based energy, one that acknowledges and answers to All That Is.

Everything we do is heart-based and, we hope, offered in a loving way.

Do you see the difference? Do you understand what it is you are striving for? Ask to become heart-centered. Along the way, many issues, people and circumstances will rise into your awareness as this clearing takes place. It is normal to cry during heart-clearing sessions, since tears are healing and must be shed in order to be released. Do not focus on the details, just focus on releasing the accumulated heartache.

In clearing heart blockages, you may witness a life-review of sorts, with a chronological pattern to those issues rising to be released. Please know that Spirit never judges, and we never attach labels of good, bad, right and wrong to those things that need releasing. We do not pry into your personal, mental or physical space. We are merely spiritual surgeons, helping you to excise the damage out of your systems. We point out here that our work together includes all aspects of both your physical half and your etheric half. This concept is new for you, since you have always considered tending to the body as tending to your whole self.

Do you now see that you must include healing of that which you cannot yet see?

AWAKENING RIGHT BRAIN
AND ALIGNING IT WITH LEFT BRAIN

The next necessary step for total assimilation is multifold in purpose. First, ask for the awakening, clearing and balancing of your right brain. Next, ask us to clear and balance your left brain. Then, ask us to realign right and left brain to work together. You see, for every step, there is a further goal. Each step that we offer you to work on is, in actuality, several steps.

First, the right brain must be reawakened. By this we mean a reawakening to active consciousness; your right brain, which connects and directs your etheric or auric self, has always been there, dutifully performing its functions. Now, we ask you to reintegrate your awareness with the right brain's functions so that you may truly become interdimensional. The parts of you which are not seen with 3D sight are invisible because why? Because those parts of you exist in higher dimensions which you cannot see, feel or connect to with your former 3D awareness. Do you see in how many different ways the ascension process is a "pulling up" of your entire existence to a higher level of consciousness?

The awakening of the right brain is a very sweet, comforting process. You will feel as if we are gently combing the right side of your head, from the mid-part outward and downward toward your ear. Each session will deepen the combing, which is occurring in 5D. Remember, the human body's essence is holographic in nature. By this we mean that any work done at the etheric level always involves the physical, because the aura and its physical core are energetically intertwined, or braided together, if you will.

Once you feel that the awakening process has deepened past the ear, it will be done. Then we will clear and rebalance your left brain, combing gently from mid-part down to the left ear. Finally, ask us to realign right brain to left brain, so that they can work together as interdependent halves of a whole. This step brings you back to original state, with left brain connected to and directing the physical half, and the right brain connected to and directing the auric half. You will find much new information coming in from your etheric self, or your auric radar, if you will. Your intuition will expand, as well as your perception of people, things, places and events that occur around you. A strong sense of peace accompanies this stage of healing, because as you begin to connect back to your aura you are consciously connecting to 5D, to higher perception, to higher mind and to us, your loving guides.

We Are One.

PHYSICAL RECONNECTION OF BODY TO AURA

Now that you have reawakened right brain and realigned it with left brain, it is time to do the same at the physical level. Ask your team of healing Brothers to consciously reconnect your body to your aura. At this stage, you are healing the depths of that major rift between Spirit energy and earth matter. You will feel a gentle tugging of, again, the mid-part line down the middle of your head, and a light pulling of it down towards your right shoulder. To balance the work, halfway through we will switch to the mid-part down over the left side of the head towards the left shoulder.

This process may take days or weeks to accomplish. The more you focus on what you are feeling, the more quickly the work proceeds. If you lose mental focus (in sessions for which you are awake) the work may slow down. The Circle of Grace will continue but will not clear as fast. That is why we say, *keep track out loud* of what you are feeling and sensing in your body and in your emotions. Remember to *open your jaw*, relax your muscles and *focus on deep breathing*. This will help you to allow the process to be guided. Since we work at all levels, we will teach you to do the same.

Always strive for balance, no matter what happens around you. At this stage, you will have the ability to deal with life best from the spiritual perspective and will instinctively know what you need to do at any given time. As this is a growth process, you may not feel major changes from day to day. But at some point you will look back to before you met us and realize how much your grasp of reality has expanded. With this spiritual growth and expansion comes an expansion of self, of blending with God, of becoming that which you seek: Wholeness is Oneness, dear ones.

FLOWERING INTO 5D SENSES

Next, ask us to help you expand into full sensory perception, what you currently term extrasensory perception. This will bring you into the bloom of 4-5D reality. Tell us, out loud, that you would like all senses, at all levels, to be opened and balanced back to your state of origin—back to your Adamic Blueprint, back to Adam Kadmon. That is your birthright, you see. What is a birthright? It is a gift or right with which you were born. You were born to be a full-sensoried, multi-dimensional, energetic creature, linked to both Father Sky and Mother Earth.

Once your senses begin to function at an expanded level, you will be able to see and counter anything of negative energy that comes around you. You will understand in a new, expansive way why people behave the way they do—because you will be able to see what "baggage" they carry around, magnetized to their auras as pockets of dense, dark matter.

Here we will remind you that *your only limits are self-imposed ones.* If you think, deep down, that none of this is possible, then it will not be possible . . . for you. So we say, use this free will zone to your advantage—turn it around and say, "God, I'm willing to believe it's all possible." Once you believe that any-thing is possible, that "the sky's the limit," then you have opened the door to your own future potential.

Do you follow?

We hope you will.

Once you have reached this level of healing, you may want to refine what you ask for, depending on the needs of your way of life or holistic practices. If you are an energetic healer, for example, you may want to request "sight" of the energies at work before you. If you are an emotional or mental healer, you might ask for clearer understanding of patterns that people work through, so as to help them identify lessons, problems, and what to do about them. If you are a spiritual healer, you might simply want to radiate higher awareness and "Be-ing-ness" wherever you go. There are as many ways to heal as there are individual people and problems, yet you all share the same elements of life, stress, activity, rest, passion, faith, etc. Healing must be accomplished at all levels, from the innermost cellular level to the outermost galactic levels. We advise you to begin in your own backyard, work on your "microcosm of the macrocosm," and know that all the rest will follow suit.

Once you have mastered this inner miracle of self-clearing, you will be in total charge of your health, your life and your future. Why? Because, no matter what happens around you, you will be in—and function from—a higher level of reality. You will, in truth, become Higher Self walking in the flesh, a true re-turn, re-membrance and re-joining of your awareness to God.

DONNING YOUR LIGHT BODY

Yes, your next request will be the fitting of your light body, which also translates to assimilating etheric and physical selves into your total Be-ing. We are very truly honored to help you don your light body. Just as the physical body has bones in it to give the body structure, your aura has a gridwork of meridian lines that form an oval-shaped energetic "cage" housing both the physical core and the internal organs of the aura. Your light body reinforces your etheric self by bringing it into wholeness with your physical core. This final merging allows Higher Self to descend and be One with you. We could fill an entire book with the explanation of how this transmutation occurs, but it would not serve our purpose here. We ask that you trust that it will be done when the time is appropriate for you.

Fitting the light body is mostly done while you are asleep, though some of you may remain semiconscious and aware of the process. The point we would like to stress here is that it does not matter whether you are aware or not; there is a progression of healing and integrating that must precede this step on the path. It is the path itself, children, that we would like you to focus on, not the details of each step that must be made. Yes, follow this list, then amend it as you see fit. Bring us your aches and pains, your questions and concepts to assimilate. It will all flow together as you begin to heal; part of your healing, you see, is shedding of old concepts, old mind-sets, to tune into the new information and the new energies coming in.

There is not enough time left to analyze every little piece of what you release and what you heal. That is the old energy, the old way. You are gaining rapid momentum and are now striding up the path at a good clip. Your light body is truly the healing and reintegrating of all of your energetic layers. Once that is complete, you will flow quite quickly through the light body assimilation. With our help, and guided by your own Higher Self, you have nothing to fear.

So, you must be asking, how will it feel? Once you have fully assimilated all aspects of your True Self, you will feel stronger, more peaceful, more focused, more patient, more benevolent, more joyful, more loving. Do you see the common word? *More.* You become more of that which you seek. You become more of all the divine aspects of Higher Self, which will be firmly in charge. You become more God-like. Yes, do you see the progression? You become more of the future potential of man.

You are evolving in this lifetime.

Dear ones, you have donned and shed those 3D bodies many times over, life after life. Now, for the first time, we ask you to bring your true Spiritual Be-ing down into that little body.

Do you follow?

We hope you will!

The donning of your light body brings a great sense of personal strength. Your physical body will feel more solid, more grounded, more balanced. Your emotions will flow through all of your layers, thought and heart added, to offer a spiritual perspective rather than an ego-based one. Be aware, dear ones, that most of you still have to deal with ego, to teach that part of you to contribute, not to guide and lead—for Spirit is leading now.

You will, at this stage, also be able to discern which people are working from ego—they will have a doom-and-gloom perspective, instill fear and give more warnings of bad than good tidings. Rely on your "gut," for your intuition will allow you to feel this negative energy as it enters your space. *That space is now a feeling part of your body.* That is your auric space, dear ones, to which you are now connected in the higher dimensions. From there, you will be able to see the lower dimensions at work around you, and you will respond from higher sight and mind.

We would like to emphasize this major point: 5D includes 3D and 4D, so you will be able to see all aspects of the dimensions you are now tuned into. From this new, higher perspective, you will clearly see what is for your highest good, and what is not. You will be in charge of your life, weighing, measuring and evaluating everything that happens around you so as to respond in harmony with your soul and its purpose.

With an integrated light body, you are carving out new heights for humanity's potential. You are, indeed, the pioneers, forging blindly into the unknown with hope and faith as fuel for advancement. You are driven by the knowing that something is missing, something essential that defines the very fabric of life that weaves together every living thing—knowledge, for sure and certain, that God exists within you.

We speak of merging here, back into All That Is. Here you will achieve the level of be-ing Godlike in every moment, recognizing that you are a part of the I AM energy. You will have bridged that gap between the free will zone and the territory it denies beyond the Veil—our realm, where every life form feels the presence of God inside them at all times.

This is, truly, becoming Higher Self. This is walking with God. This is the waking meditation that we offer to teach you. Yes, the Circle of Grace helps to clear you and get you ready. It also does one vital thing more—it reconnects your inner hope and faith, you see, with the sure knowledge that God exists. You will feel God living inside of you, once again.

CARE AND MAINTENANCE OF THE AURA

All we advise you to ask for in this chapter should become for you a sequence of both self-healing and maintenance. By this we mean that you should, every once in a while, repeat questions #1-5 as listed at the end of this chapter. Ask to be repolarized, ask for your meridians and chakras to be cleared and balanced. Ask for heart to be cleared. While you live, breathe and function in your everyday world, there is always a new accumulation of stress and pain incoming to your system. So, not only do we counsel you to work through these steps towards wholeness, we say to you, the Circle of Grace should be as much a part of your daily physical maintenance as showering and brushing your teeth. Do it every day, or as often as possible. Go to sleep at night floating on the awareness that your body is clearing, where it is happening, and what that means to you.

Please remember that the Circle of Grace is also for current maintenance and clearing. In other words, each time you lie down to do the exercise you will be clearing at two levels— that of current stress and strain, and the level of past (accumulated) stress and strain. If a session feels different than what you requested, know that we must finish clearing the way before we can move on with new work. *We must work from the outside in.* The Circle of Grace clears from the outside in. The deeper the clearing, the older and heavier the baggage. At the physical level, the outer layers of chronic pain must be released before the deeper source of the blockage or emotional damage can be reached for healing.

Some days, the earth's energy shifts will be so heavy and draining that you will want nothing more than added energy.

Ask (aloud) for energy when you need it, and let us gauge how much to feed you. At first, you will feel as if unending waves of goose bumps are washing over your body. That is energizing at the physical level. As you advance and your requests gain complexity, you will often need to find surcease in 5D, the energy to which you are being drawn.

On those days, for those who can handle it, you will feel as if you are being dipped in a big vat of rainbows. You will grow to see the rich palate of colors that vibrate in 5D as your senses expand. Others will feel a warm, loving darkness aglow with inner light. Some will hear frequency changes in the form of tones ringing in their ears. Again, each person will have individual experiences, tailored to their need for healing, learning and growing back into their original perspective of blending with Higher Self.

We work with each of you independently, so what one person experiences will not necessarily match another. Also, know that we tailor the work to suit your goals and spiritual life path. Remember, in the Healing Prayer, that you ask your own Higher Self to guide and lead? There is good reason for that request—all that we do is tailored to what your Higher Self directs us to do according to your soul contract, for your highest good, in Divine Timing.

As to Divine Timing, some of you may find yourselves in a headlong struggle with timing. By this we mean that your impatience to move forward can sometimes get in your way. If you ask us to continue to another step before we feel that you are ready, we cannot move on without risking you harm. Please understand that from our 5D perspective we see your past, present and future, and thus see the ramifications of each request. If you feel stuck or blocked in your progress and cannot understand why, know that you are "being held in place" by Spirit, protected until you are ready to move forward safely.

As you reach a level of comfortable usage of the Circle of Grace, you will have the ability to ask for and receive more than one focus at a time. For example, you could ask for an energy bath and drain out a headache, at the same time. Once you can recognize what each step of this process feels like, you can activate it by connecting with us and bringing in the feel of it.

Through all of this work, we hope that you will lie down and try the exercise. The proof is in the doing, and you have nothing to lose except many layers of pain and stress!

REACHING WHOLENESS

Asking for all of the healing listed here at once is too much to focus on. Each level must be cleared before the next level can be reached for healing. We offer the information in this chapter for your assimilation, to help speed your progress up the path. Knowing what to ask for makes the work much simpler for us all, and we feel it is time that this knowledge be brought forth before the Veil.

Once you understand the path of healing that needs to be followed, you can tailor your requests to suit your individual needs. This chapter contains the basic steps for you to follow in healing at all levels. Do not limit yourself to this list. See it rather as the foundation of our collaboration, for as you live and grow your needs will change and thus guide our future work.

We urge you not to measure your Circle of Grace sessions against the progress of another person. Each will be different, no better or worse, just different. This is not a race of any kind—we ask you to reach awareness in your own time, in your own way. That is following highest good, Divine Timing, under grace, within the Circle of Grace.

Once you have felt us work on you, there is no turning back. Even if you were to cry from the rooftops, "There is no God," you would not believe, in those depths that we touched, that God does not exist. We exist, dear ones, a mere breath away from you, only a few octaves above you, yet we can, with your verbal permission, reach through that gap and touch you. We are waiting to work with you, with all awakening and aware ones, creating as we go a new wave of evolved humanity. One by one, you will begin to bring in "channels" that no one else gets. You will gain healing and knowledge and total love in this work. You will pave the way for others to follow, an ever-increasing flood of people awakening to Spirit as your galaxy draws nearer to the photon belt.

All of the planets in your solar system are now showing marked changes in luminosity, changes in polarity, changes in gravitational fields and atmospheric conditions. When we tell you that all is changing around you, that "All" is beyond huge!

When one level shifts, all levels must shift.

This shift will bring in your ultimate goal—reconnection to God. That is the ultimate goal of the Divine plan for humanity, you see, for you to find your inner Divine flame, to choose to return to God of your own free will. Ah, now we come to the crux of the meaning of all the goals. And you already know what that is:

I Am GOD. You Are GOD. We Are GOD. We Are ONE.

In the healing of your bodies and your reawakening to your original powers, you will, indeed, change the tapestry of all creation. We are honored and humbled to be working with you, dear ones, you who bear such heavy loads. Know that there is more to life than you see. Know that you are all, one and all, beloved. You are beloved of God, you sprang from God and will find your way back to God in a new and different way—as evolved, blended beings—as the New Humans in this, the New Age of Humanity.

Welcome Home.

List of Questions to Ask the Brothers In Healing Sessions

1) Repolarization—ask to be repolarized at all levels
2) Clear & balance energetic meridians
3) Clear & balance energy centers (chakras)
4) Clear & balance lower three chakras to upper three, with heart as new fulcrum
5) Clear & balance physical heart chakra to Spiritual Heart chakra
6) Awaken, clear & balance right brain
7) Clear & balance left brain
8) Align left & right brain together
9) Physical reconnection of body to aura
10) Flower gently into 5D senses
11) Bring in my light body
12) Care and maintenance of the aura

*Please Note: For **maximum** effectiveness, these stages of healing are meant to be done in the order that they are presented here.*

The Brotherhood Healing Prayer

In order to form a physical link with your personal group of Brothers, please say this four-part prayer out loud before you begin a Circle of Grace session:

Call upon Father/Mother God, Creator of all that is, was, and ever will be, to join you in the healing session.

Call upon your favorite Ascended Masters, guides, angels, and religious figure(s), whomever you hold dear, to join you in the healing session.

Call upon us, the Brotherhood of Light, to join you in the healing session.

Call upon your own soul, or Higher Self, to join you and guide the healing session.

Tell us what you wish to focus on, either from the list of questions we have provided or specific personal issues (physical or conceptual.) The vibration of your voice bridges the dimensions, giving us the permission we need to interact with you in your free will zone, to work on you in your own physical space.

Do you follow?

We hope you will!

We are, in All Love, the Brotherhood of Light

Section Two

The Universal Laws

Chapter Six

The Law of Materialization

In this chapter, we wish to discuss the nature of your reality. You probably know by now that reality is a variable thing. Most of you feel that it is beyond your control. Things "just happen" to you. Life has constant twists and turns that you find unexpected and not always welcome. We say to you here that *reality is in your control*. You have been in control of your lives and your reality all along, you just didn't know it. If you understand the workings of the universe, you will then be able to manipulate your reality, and your lives, as you wish.

Or rather, as you will.

LEARNING TO WIELD YOUR WILL

There are aspects of "free will" that you are graced with that separate you from other schools (i.e., planets) of spiritual learning. You probably think having free will means that believing or not believing in God is your choice, as is how you believe, as well. Yes, you are absolutely right on both counts, but free will means much more than that.

Free will also means that you can "wield your will" in any way you choose. You have incredible powers of will, as is proven by the communal reality you live in. You have all agreed to live in the matrix of 3D, a construct of physical reality

through which you translate into a physical body, over and over
again, in order to learn lessons at the physical level. Your world
is a created one, one that you all share and see. Though each
individual has his or her own perceptions about 3D reality, you
all basically see the same things—roads, buildings, trees, animals and plants. This construct is so strong that the births and
deaths of its inhabitants do not affect its existence.

Here we will state: *you create what you focus on.* Put another
way—a change of perspective, if you will—the universe brings
to you what you hold most in your awareness. Have you known
people who were afraid of illnesses like cancer, only to die of
it? The more they focused on what they feared, the more the
universe delivered it. Do you focus on lack in your life? Then
the universe will bring you lack, since that is your focus.
Rather, focus on what you do have, and be grateful for the sustenance and abundance that flows around you. Then the universe will bring you abundance from all around.

You may be thinking, easy to say and hard to do. Is it? Not
really. **The Law of Manifestation states that you create
what you focus your awareness on.** If you feel convinced
of something down to your bones, is it not easier to manifest
than if you just feel ambivalent toward it? In other words, the
more intensely you wield your will, the better and faster creation you achieve of what you want. People who succeed are
those who never take their eyes off their goal. When you focus
on and acknowledge limitations and obstacles to your goal,
they then appear to you because that is where your put your
attention, your focus or your sight.

You only see obstacles when you take your eyes off your goal.

How to do this correctly? How to obtain your heart's
desire? The strongest of intent is that which is funneled
through the heart. If you are doing your heart's true work, the
universe will support your efforts. As we have said before, follow your heart. Let your heart be your guide. Run every
thought, idea and sentence through the heart chakra before
you bring it into your current 4D reality with the power of
your voice.

Yes, your voice has much power. Your voice carries your hopes, wishes, dreams, thoughts and ideas into materialization through the power of verbalizing—*what you speak becomes concrete.* In this text, we are already teaching you how to do this! By saying the four-part Healing Prayer aloud before each Circle of Grace session, you are creating a bridge between dimensions and giving us permission to work with you in your physical space.

Voicing your will brings your creation down into the physical level of your reality. Yes, dear ones, affirmations done over and over, joyously from the heart, are very powerful! The auditory vibration of your voice is your best creative tool to wield the will of your heart and mind. That is why we urge you to speak aloud to us during our healing sessions together, even though you may not see, hear or feel us yet. Do you see your enormous potential in the word "yet"? We do, and we honor you greatly for it.

KNOW THAT ANYTHING IS POSSIBLE

What we are focusing our attention on here is the concept of manifestation (chuckle). How to create what you want, how to make your goal(s) a reality, how to create and earn abundance by following your inherent gifts and talents, accumulated through many lifetimes. We urge you to see your lessons now as merely obstacles on your path and to look beyond them to your goal. We seek to facilitate your clearing of all obstacles in your life that impede your progress back to All That Is. It is time now for intense soul work, to identify and follow the spiritual contract you charted for yourself before you incarnated into this body and into this life.

Interesting concept, isn't it? In the previous chapter, we offered you a list of things to ask for in our healing sessions together. Why? The key words here are "what to ask for." The universe provides you with what you ask for, or what you focus your attention on. *We, the Melchizedek Brotherhood, can only do what you ask us to do.* Knowing what to ask for is crucial to this entire process, for there is a logical progression to the unfolding, or flowering, of the transitions from 3D to 4D to 5D. There is a flow of physical, emotional, mental and spiritual (PEMS) transitions that you must follow in order to translate into the higher realms. Please remember, too, that the list is merely a road map, a pattern that you can amend or adjust to suit your individual needs.

We ask you to keep in mind that nothing is impossible.

This basic tenet must, by logic and necessity, be true for you down to your bones. Even if you grasp all of the concepts that the New Age material offers, none of it will help you to evolve if you do not believe in your own power and potential. Please note here that we are not trying to dictate to you what or how you should or should not believe. That would be in conflict with your free will directive.

Believe in whatever source of religion feels right to you, knowing that all viable religions preach the same message of love, not hate. By staying open to infinite possibilities, you are allowing Spirit to bring in the highest and best for you, as directed by the universe (or your personal identification of God) under grace, in Divine Timing.

What do we mean by this? We mean simply that whatever you seek, wish or focus on to create, say it aloud with this phrase interwoven: "...for my highest good, under grace and in Divine Timing." Focus on the goal rather than a specific path to that goal. Thus you allow the universe to work in myriad ways, instead of limiting yourself to a single outcome through a single (stated) path. There may be many possibilities out there that will bring your desire into better fruition, but if you specify too much, you are limiting yourself (and us) as to what you can receive. Trust that we, from Spirit's higher perspective, have a clearer view of what constitutes your highest good, as well as how and when it should happen.

So, state the problem (out loud!) and specify your desired goal. Here is where discernment comes in—as you limit yourself by choosing only one path toward a goal, you must carefully phrase your goal requirements so that it brings you all that you wish to manifest. If you pray for enough food to feed your family, and then complain that you have little more than food to survive, we will gently say, *"Your prayer has been answered."* Rather, ask for enough abundance to sustain your family and share with your friends, and see what that expansion in perspective and prayer brings into your life!

Here is another example of being specific in creating your goals. As you work with us toward the upward expansion of your senses, we will teach you how to "phase in and out" of 5D sight, so that you will be in control of what you see, when you wish to see it. Think of it as an "on-off switch," if you like. You won't want to be "seeing" all the time, for it would be too great a distraction and it would interfere with how you interact with others. Here is where we reiterate, be careful what you wish for!

Be specific in the goal you seek, by imagining yourself already there. See yourself beyond mastery, already using your gifts, and that "future vision" will show you exactly what you will need to bring in. How to achieve mastery, how to get there, is easy—do the Circle of Grace, tell us aloud what you seek, and allow us to worry about the refinements of your goals, gifts and talents.

CREATING MASTERY THROUGH HEALTH AT ALL LEVELS

The Law of Materialization is very important for you to understand, because you are creatures of materialization. Visualized prayers are the fuel for creating and manifesting your work on earth. This is how you learn and grow, and gain more and more control over your life, your future and your time. Learn to balance your time. By this we mean, many of you work beyond the body's endurance, eat poorly, sleep poorly, and then wonder why you feel poorly! Sit down and take a long, hard look at how you treat your body—it is your vehicle for soul expression in this life.

You have set schedules and laws built around the maintenance of your cars, needing inspections and tune-ups and oil changes. You need to do the same with your own vehicle! Your bodies deserve preventative maintenance care, too. We ask you to honor all of it, the spiritual and the scientific. Again, they are two sides of the same coin. That coin represents the totality of "knowingness"—what we in Spirit know and what you as humans have learned about yourselves. Use the scientific technology available to you, plus the help we offer, to stay clear and balanced. In other words, be aware of what your total being (not just your physical body) needs to be healthy.

How to achieve and maintain health? Through the consistent use of the Circle of Grace. Call upon us to help you, that is what we are waiting for. Set up a ritual, something that carries meaning for you. Spirit honors rituals, for they show the intensity of your intent, your focus and commitment to all that you do. Ask us what you want, thank us for taking care of it and *feel grateful for having the fruition of your desires as if it had already happened.* The intensity of that feeling of gratitude is what propels materialization. Yes, yes, pass it through your hearts! Pray from the heart, visualize your desire through the heart, give thanks from the heart, and release it to the universe. Your desire will shoot straight up like an arrow, an arrow that is guaranteed to hit its mark even as it is released.

Do you follow?

We hope you will.

Please keep in mind that the Circle of Grace is an active meditation. It is an exercise in expanding your focus inward that propels your awareness up to the higher realms. If you do not wish to meditate, see this process as a self-clearing and self-maintaining exercise, akin to taking walks or lifting weights. If you do not wish to exercise, see the Circle of Grace as an expansion of awareness that enhances your life at all levels, from the deepest physical levels to the highest metaphysical levels. Do you thus understand that we wish to include all of you? We hope that you will someday use this exercise as an important step in your daily self-maintenance.

BECOMING THAT WHICH YOU SEEK

We offer here again a spiritual nutshell view mentioned in the first chapter: In prayer you speak to God, in meditation you listen to God. Here we may add: In the Circle of Grace, you interact with God to bring in mastery of your self-healing, which is your evolutionary birthright ripening in Divine Timing now! We invite you, dear ones, to co-create a new reality with us (chuckle).

For true, total metaphysical advancement, this is what is required: A change in your perspective of who and what you are. Your bodies may return to the earth over and over, but your consciousness infinitely returns to the True Reality of Spirit. You need to release your old 3D human view of limited life in limited bodies. *You need to begin seeing yourselves as Eternal Be-ings—energetic beings with temporary physical cores.*
You never die, dear ones. And you are never alone!
From this shift in perspective comes an expanded realization of your self-worth, and your divine right to become the expanded being inherent in your potential. A "knowing" will grow in you of your true powers to direct and affect this life, and all lives, that you have experienced. Then you will fully become an eternal, energetic being wielding your will— through the power of loving gratitude—to create your desire, your goal and hence your future reality.

In the beginning, the most difficult part will be learning how to put aside the cares and worries of your "mundane life," and float up into the higher energy levels that we represent and offer here to share with you. In our healing sessions together, remember to speak aloud to us of your hopes, wishes and dreams, and we will care for them as if they were the finest of jewels. We care for you, too, more than you can know at present!

We wait impatiently for your return to the True Reality of Spirit. In whatever manner your journey unfolds, we care not. All is perfect, the good and the bad, the mistakes and the triumphs, the choices made and those not made. Remember, in our eyes, you cannot do it wrong (re: each lifetime) for there are concrete reasons behind everything that happens, reasons you may not see or understand yet from your linear 3–4D perspective.

Know that each lifetime unravels as it must, with lessons learned and wisdom gained.

What is it you gain from all of this work? A chance never possible for humans before. You have reached "maturity" as a species, which means that it is time for you to evolve to the next stage. Evolve into what? Fifth-dimensional human beings.

Your senses, talents and gifts will increase exponentially in the next ten years [channeled August 2001]. We say here to those of you who seek and practice this metaphysical work and others like it—you are shifting first, the first wave to stay and shift, to anchor the Higher Light in your bodies before the general population. Most of you will shift between 2004 and 2008. By then, you will have established your new, higher energetic "balance" and clearly marked the road for others to follow.

Yes, all who are awakened are aware of the projected 2012 marker as the ascension point of earth. This "zero-point" will be near the end of the year 2012 for, if you remember, the Chinese, and Spirit, count the one-year marker at the end of the year, not the beginning. What will happen then? That future reality (and the ultimate date of the earth's shift) is still shaping itself, energized by all of you who focus on love and learning. Your fuel? Intent. Desire. Love.

Think about this: You come into this world naked and empty-handed. You leave this world without possessions, without even a body. So what is the purpose of all this karmic journeying? Why are you "doomed," as some of you think, to repeat life after life and be miserable because that is the "human condition"?

We say to you here that your human condition is whatever you want it to be. Your life is and will be whatever you want it to be, whatever you focus on the most. You were put on this earth to experience freedom and joy. Your true soul-directed goals are creating love and attaining wisdom. Those are the two priceless things that you take back to your true Spirit life. These are the treasures of the soul: Becoming love and wisdom, becoming thy full potential, God-self incarnate in flesh. Through the ascension process, your goal is to cleanse and purify all aspects of self so that you may merge back into the Godhead. By this we mean whatever concept you have of God, whether it be Christ, Adonai, Allah, Buddha or simply the Universe.

Can you imagine this? A return to the warmth and love of the Divine Creator, the Father/Mother energy that flows through All That Is. Imagine yourself, your awareness of body, mind and soul, merging with a glorious rainbow of incredible energy that permeates and sustains all dimensional realities. You are not merely a spark of God; you carry the divine flame in every cell of your body. That divine flame is what fuels your existence. Once you purify and integrate all aspects of your total being, your Higher Self will be able to descend and blend with you. You will live from that moment on with a live, active, permanent knowledge that God exists, for you will feel His presence as a new, specific vibration inside your body.

Once you achieve oneness with Spirit, all will change for you. For some, it will be a clear and incisive moment. For others, it will build slowly and transition slowly—one day, you will realize that you have become self-realized (chuckle)! Some people will never understand, or even know, that anything is happening. They will change the most slowly, accommodating the new energy as best they can without conscious awareness of the process. Many will fall ill as the planetal frequency rises beyond what their bodies can match. Some will translate over and come home to us through the doorway of death. Some will experience life-changing events that will plunk them on the spiritual path like lost lambs looking for a warm barn.

We remind you that each person will come to self-awareness in his or her own time. *Lightworkers, work on yourselves. Work on each other—we cannot stress this enough.* It is vital to match emotional, mental and spiritual development with physical and psychic development. How to accomplish this? Join with us through the exercise we offer, the Circle of Grace. By working together we can clear and balance you to a higher frequency of energetic expression. If you are ill, we can augment and quicken your healing.

We can also help prevent medical complications by guiding the doctors' minds and hands as they work on you. Call us in as you would for a healing session, and we will accompany you to the doctor's office, even into surgery. From our place in the Now of True Reality, we can be with you in your linear time frame as often as you call upon us.

See your entire life as one big healing session for your ascent to a new way of being, and we will gladly journey there with you! Again, we stress the mental awareness of "Be-ing" in

every moment. We add here, be with us! Let us be with you.
Think in terms of God being within you and surrounding you,
with every stride and in every moment that you breathe in and
out on this earth. Do not think of God as above or at a dis-
tance, not noticing or caring about you—that could not be further from the truth. *You are God.* God is All That Is, and you
are part of All That Is!

BE-ING IN LOVE WITH LIFE

Do you see the layers upon layers of patterns in your life,
and how one flows to the next? Consider this: Yes, the end
result of each life is bringing back to Spirit more love and wisdom, but for you now that is not the most important part to
focus on. *Now, we ask you simply to enjoy the journey.* Each lifetime should be a joyous expression of God in the material
dimension, not an experience of pain and suffering.

Do you understand that you have a choice in this? Yes, a
lovely aspect of free will is that you can choose a perspective,
amend it to suit your needs or discard it for a better one.
Remember, you create your own reality in every moment that
you live and breathe. Look around at your present life—it is
the sum total of all that you have created in the past. Look at
what you are creating now as you work each day—it will
become your future reality!

In this time of transition, you have been granted the dispensation of moving quickly forward on the spiritual path. You no
longer need to endure long periods of pain and suffering; that
was the old energy, the old human mindset. Now you can identify and assimilate the lesson that each experience carries and
walk through it! Get past it! Let go of the past! How, you ask?

The old human expression, "Forgive and forget," is truer
than you know. Forgive, yes, to clear your karmic slate and
allow you clear focus for the here and now. Forget, yes, in the
sense that you should not dwell on the past. By focusing on
past mistakes and painful events you are putting your awareness, and therefore your energy, in the wrong place. As we
explained in prior text, your spiritual layer records everything

that occurs to you in each life, and how you respond. That part, you see, is taken care of. Do not get caught up in mental loops that drain you of vital energy and get you nowhere; instead, let go of it all, and float up with us into the healing energies of the Circle of Grace.

Clear and balance, clear and balance. That is what we offer to help you with, a direct path to all of your physical and metaphysical goals. The Circle of Grace is your vehicle to moving forward; by its use, you move your physical vehicle forward!

YOU ARE NOT ALONE, YOU ARE ALL ONE

We, the Brotherhood of Light, are spiritual surgeons and material mechanics, here to offer explanations of how things work. How the universe works, and how you can use the universal laws to shape your reality. How you can deepen and enrich your lives by including the Circle of Grace. This exercise is not just an exercise, not just a meditation—that is just the mode in which you experience it. The Circle of Grace is your internal self-clearing system, present in each and every one of you. And we offer it here as a present to you from Spirit!

Why not learn to use it?

Do you not say that for every illness, God put on this earth a plant that can cure it? Indeed, He has done even more than that. Your physical bodies are a brilliant creation of physical matter married to spiritual matter. You have discovered only a small understanding of the complexities of your own biological systems. Does it not make sense that the incredible biological creature that you are would have a built-in way of maintaining and regaining health?

You will find God in the divine perfection of every detail of life. The Circle of Grace covers all the details and all the levels for you, in one simple exercise. We cannot stress this enough: *Ascension work must be done at all levels, including the physical.* Would you take off across the ocean in a flimsy, leaky boat? Of course not, you know that you would never survive the trip. Do you see? In order to accomplish the full transition gracefully, you must be clear and balanced at all levels. Give intent to do the work, take the time to lie down and connect with us, and you will not be disappointed.

How will you know when you have successfully transitioned? How will you know when you get there? You will find us waiting! Then your true life path unfolds as you begin to fulfill the higher contract written by your soul. Then you will have a new set of goals to go along with the new set of tools that you have developed. Your entire Be-ing, mind, body and Spirit, will form a phenomenal spiritual tool that you will wield with steadfast faith and sharp intent—what a powerful combination! Your human ability to focus will come now into play, for with evolved faith, intent and focus, you can create anything that you can imagine. That is why we say to you, ***Believe that any thing is possible.*** Otherwise, you will be self-limiting.

Many things will flower from your final transition to 5D. This is your graduation, dear ones, from the karmic cycle of earth. Above you, a whole new set of dimensions will open up. You will be asked, how would you like to serve the Divine Plan? In body or in Spirit? In which dimension, or set of dimensions? Working at the physical or spiritual level of connection? Do you wish to continue serving humanity, or do you wish to translate into another school of teaching, another planet and a new spiritual configuration?

Your true potential is as vast as All There Is. In the microcosm that is a human being is reflected the macrocosm that is God. We are All One in Spirit. However it is that you see us, whether it is as the Brotherhood of Light, the (Great) White Brotherhood, or the Order of Melchizedek, it matters not. We are all part of the spiritual hierarchy, serving the greater good and the Divine Plan. You, too, in the flesh now, are part of this majestic reality that is the true nature of God. You are at the physical level, where things really happen. You are the core fighters, the front line of evolution in this part of the multiverses of universes that comprise All That Is. We honor you greatly for this "heavy duty" you have assumed.

Please understand that it is our wish to work with you in whatever form of spiritual, mental, emotional or physical healing you may need. You will make quick progress in our healing sessions together if you motivate this work with your spiritual quests for love and learning. If you have trouble connecting with us, read any part of the material we offer here, and you will plow a path straight to our energetic signature.

Through this work, these are our goals for you: Learn how to use the Circle of Grace. Learn how your energetic body works to heal your - self. Learn to control all aspects of your reality, internal and external and thus advance gracefully into becoming a conscious, blended being of Spirit and Matter.

We are honored to offer our help, especially now as you begin to flower into new senses. Bring us your aching heart, and we will gently minister to it. Bring us your fears and doubts, and we will release them for you. Visualize release during the Circle of Grace exercise, see the murky golden liquid in your meridians flow through and out, carrying away your pain and stress. Replace that tainted energy with new, bright, gold-white universal energy that is your etheric food. Lightworkers, learn how to get clear and stay clear. Help each other to reach clarity, so that you will be ready to help others who follow behind you on the path back to wholeness.

Be open. Be receptive. Be with us, and you will soon join us. And what a party we have planned! Your return is always a joyous occasion for us, whether you come Home in Spirit, or visit with us in body. How? Join us in the Circle of Grace. Be a part of the evolution of man. Clear yourselves so that Higher Self can join you in the joyous expression of your life on earth.

We know you can do this, for we know that anything is possible!

Chapter Seven

The Law of Allowing

In this chapter, we would like to focus on another universal law, the Law Of Allowing. We have already discussed the concept of the Law Of Materialization, which states that you create in your 4D reality that on which you focus your attention. If you focus on what you lack, that is what you will create. If you focus on what you love, that is what you will create.

The Law Of Allowing is simply this: *You create what you focus on and allow to bring into your universe.* Each man is a universe unto himself, complete and whole as created by God. To think you are lacking in anything defiles the model upon which you were created—the spark of divinity. We keep repeating in this text that "You are God," do we not? If, indeed, you are part of the I Am energy, then it stands to reason that you have available to you God's powers of creation! Why do we phrase it thus? Because of the parameters of your free-will zone. You are as powerful as you believe yourself to be. You are as aware as you choose to be. You are as worthy as you feel yourself to be. You are as loved as you love yourself.

Along with knowledge and wisdom gained, these are the treasures that your soul seeks in each lifetime: Self-worth leading to self-love, higher awareness and return to the I Am consciousness. Since you are currently confined to a physical body, these soul experiences must be cultivated at the physical level. Your daily work helps to define your self-worth. Your emotional relationships reflect the depths of your self-love. Your application of higher mental perspective to your daily life will show as success at all levels. When your faith in God becomes faith in yourself, you will discover your boundless power of co-creation on the physical plane. Yes, you can and will create your own future, step by step, as you begin to positively change your current life and see proof that you can affect all that is around you.

CREATING YOUR FUTURE REALITY

This is how you create your reality: First you hone your focus on a specific goal, then you will your creation into physicality through loving gratitude, then you step aside and allow the goal to materialize. How do you allow? By willing it. Your "will" has many facets: The will to focus your intent, the will to create your goal, the will to allow that creation into your Now. Again, you are creatures of free will, and you have the capacity, talent and power to create whatever you will (chuckle). Use your will like a finely-honed sword, to point at that which you desire, then focus on it to the exclusion of all else. Once you have achieved total focus, you must then will your goal into existence.

How? Send it up to Spirit as a prayer from the heart, fueled by your gratitude for having that prayer answered. Then you must detach from that prayer, move aside and allow it to become realized. How to let it go? Allowing is a release of your prayer, like an arrow shot of your will, directed by the fuel of your faith. You must release it, so that it can fly free in order to reach its mark. If you continue holding on to it with worry and doubt, it will by necessity stop flying and return back to you, which is not pleasant and certainly does not achieve your goal. So graciously allow it to fly free, release it and detach from the outcome. By allowing, by stepping aside, you are giving space in your 4D world for your manifestation to land and appear. Yes, like a big package!

So, what do you do next, as you wait for your goal to materialize? Keep allowing for it to happen! Keep your intent pure, function from your higher perspective by maintaining your focus on being the ultimate Creator Be-ing that you are. Here we remind you, as explained in the previous chapter on the Law Of Materialization, to keep your attention on your goal rather than try to plan or fret over how it will come in. By trying to guess how your materialization will manifest, you are limiting yourself as to what and how you can receive, and also limiting the ways in which Spirit can help bring it in for you.

Become your goal. Try it on for size. Look around, and see what tools you will need as you function after realizing your goal. Bring together all of those tools, and create a sacred space in which to place your materialization. In other words, *start preparing for your goal as if it were already here, and keep giving thanks for its creation.*

Defining the tools that you will need is part of your creative manifestation. What will you need to work within your goal after it has arrived? If it is a business, you will need business cards, stationery, a system of bookkeeping. Where will the business be located? Pick an area in which you feel comfortable working. Design your office space, see the colors of the walls and rugs, decide what type of furniture will suit your needs, down to the material (metal? wood?) and color of your desk. Perfection is in the smallest details. Figure it all out, and trust that Spirit will bring it to you in Divine Timing, under grace, and for your highest good.

WHAT YOU WANT IS ALREADY DONE

Dear one, are you still asking, "But how do I do it? How do I will what I want into existence?" Our answer is simply, "By imagining it already done." The human mind is a wondrous thing—it does not distinguish between what is real and what is imagined, it functions only on data input. So, you can dream your goal into being! See it done. Imagine yourself beyond the manifestation of it, see yourself working within your goal. Look around. What do you need to do the goal's work? What will you need to implement that goal?

Prepare as if your heart's desire has already arrived. Keep sending love and gratitude from the heart, thanks to Spirit for having accomplished the goal. All the while, gather your tools.

Make them, if you can, so that you can hold them in your hands. Or imagine them in your life, see yourself using them, see yourself functioning as if your goal had already arrived. *Put your awareness beyond getting the goal into having the goal.* Function as if it were done. Be there, taste it, feel it, see it in your mind's eye, and it will catch up to you.

Do you follow?

We hope you will.

How this is done is moment by moment. Put yourself into the "mental groove" of gratitude for the goal accomplished, and when you stray from that perspective, pull yourself back into it. Pretty soon, you will be functioning at a higher level of awareness and creativity that will accomplish any goal that you seek.

To summarize: Your physical body anchors the thought, the idea, the goal. Your emotional body gives the fuel of living grace to that which you have established as your goal. Then the mental body refines the plan, fleshing out the desire into the needed components that you intend to materialize. Then your spiritual layer takes the whole package, like a slingshot, and sends it straight up from your heart to the heart of God. So, define your goal, see it already alive, send it up with gratitude and thanks, then get busy creating your tools as you allow your manifestation to materialize. That is the order in which you must work.

SUSTAINING A HIGHER ENERGETIC VIBRATION

Please keep in mind that all forms of life are expressions of specific vibratory energy. You are energetic beings, holographic in design, whose powers extend far further than you realize. Indeed, your bodies are much larger than you realize, and function at many more levels than you are aware of. *Any change that you choose to implement in your physical reality requires first a vibrational shift of your energy.*

Your physical core is the last and deepest level to be shifted.

Remember how we explained in Chapter 5 that the Circle of Grace process must first clear your outer layers of pain and stress before the inner layers can be reached for release? In the ascension process, you also change from the outside in—first your spiritual body, then mental, then emotional and, last, your physical body. How do you make each shift? By changing your perspective! When we say, "Seek a higher perspective," we are asking you to access a higher level of vibratory expression— that is what "raising your consciousness" is all about! The "allowing" part of manifestation is *sustaining* that higher vibration. By making that higher perspective your true inner expression, you develop the power to positively affect the vibrational density of your physical reality.

In order to sustain that higher level of awareness consciousness, it is not necessary to focus on the goal you seek in every moment that you breathe. Indeed, you would not be able to function in your everyday world with such a narrow mental focus. Rather, we mean that you should seek to sustain the feeling of faith, the positive outpouring of love, to maintain your being at all levels in a state of Oneness with the Divine Source. Do not retreat into fear, worry and doubt, for these negative thought forms drag you back down into density. Remember that you have, in every moment, the choice to be in fear or in love. Simply choose the higher vibration of love, and do not allow anything or any one around you to lower your essence back down into density and duality. Sustaining your faith and your positive perspective will magnetize your goal to you, as long as you believe and allow that anything is possible.

ALLOWING YOUR FAITH TO COME FROM YOUR HEART

How do you allow? We do not speak here of clenching your gut or holding your breath, or doing anything physical to bring your desires into realization. You must be self-realized in order to realize, or materialize, things (chuckle). How to become self-realized? Through the state of grace achieved by mastering the Circle of Grace within you.

Do you see the many layers of this work? To be self-realized is to be aware, in every moment, of your connection to Higher Self. *You must totally believe in your divinity, in your power as*

Creator. Doing the Circle of Grace regularly will become the
inner core of your faith, your connection to and your proof
that God resides within you. Then you will find it easy to
believe in the power of your will to create that which you
desire from the depths of your heart.

We say, always lead with your heart. The heart is the fulcrum upon which your entire being is balanced. It is the axis of
your will, the lens of your soul, that you use to focus on your
physical reality. That which you desire from the depths of your
heart you will create the best. That which you *attempt* to create
with ambivalence, or lack of caring, will not manifest. That
which you create through the negative emotions of fear, in all
of its faces, will also descend upon you with its own brand of
lessons in tow.

That which you send out, you receive back threefold.

Do you see your higher purpose now? Do that which you
focus on. Be that which you intend to become. Walk your talk.
Begin to merge with All That Is, and carry His awareness in
every moment that you breathe. Once you give thanks to
Spirit, with love and gratitude pouring from your heart chakra,
then see it as already done, and will it, so be it. Sounds simple?
Yes, surely. But you must release personal ego, or you will get
in your own way.

GETTING OUT OF YOUR OWN WAY

Surrendering ego is what you face at this level of metaphysical learning. Let go of that voice which argues against your own
heart, that inner voice of lower thought that belittles the divinity that you are, by negating that Spirit exists inside you. It is
the voice that keeps insisting that not everything is possible.

Do you see? It is the voice of duality. It is the voice of human
tribal thought, which tries to control your thinking and your
actions. It is the voice that diminishes your self-worth. It is time
to step away from that limiting voice, away from that limited
mode of thinking. It is time to stand up as an individual, with
your own unique set of inner beliefs and outward expressions.

How to attain self-worth and not have an overblown ego?
That is your current quandary. In human terms, overfocus on

selfish gain interferes with your dedication to Higher Self. We hope to help you grow past ego-definition through your awakening, and now your awareness, of All That Is. Then you will define your self-worth from a spiritual perspective rather than a material perspective. You will grow into the realization that polishing your inside is more essential than polishing your outside!

Keep in mind that the goal of Higher Self is to seek love and wisdom in each lifetime. Your self-worth is not predicated upon how many material possessions you pile up around you—remember, you leave all that behind. That success is good, yes, and necessary to insure the survival of your physical core on earth. But many of you never stop focusing on those material goods and elevate their status to that of divine worth. That is not so. That is not true.

The real value of each lifetime is how much divinity you discover within yourself, and how much you yearn to get the work done so you can go Home! Yet, if you embrace this yearning as the be-all of your existence, you will find yourself clutching a bouquet filled with hidden thorns. Yes, it is important to have that yearning, for it paves your path with solid advancement. But if you focus too much on just one part of this process, you will become stuck there.

What if your heart's desire doesn't manifest right away? We say, remember Divine Timing. Also remember that the little voice of doubt that repeats that question, and others like it, are of the lower mind. Again, this is a facet of free will—choose the higher vibration of love, in every moment, rather than the lower vibration of fear in all of its faces. Stay in higher mind, in a loving vibration, *in an attitude of gratitude that will make your life a beatitude.*

Doubt is partner to fear, and fear blocks. Now is the time to tear down those blocks, toss them aside and stride right by. You have this time of planetary dispensation and the tools to prepare yourself. Make the Circle of Grace part of your daily routine, to prepare yourself at all levels for the fabulous times ahead.

Value yourself for being a spark of God. That is your shining glory, your raison d'etre in every life on your plane of existence. Through life after life in the material world, you are asked to rediscover your slumbering connection to God, your inner flame that is God Light in your body. You must find and reach that light through the heart, not the intellect. Reach it, establish it, and nurture it through the healing energies of the Circle of Grace. We say to you here, you have always been and will always be one-on-one with God. Your current duality is the false reality. Our reality is the true Home of your Eternal Spirit, where you return after each set of life lessons.

WHICH CAME FIRST, THE SOIL OR THE SEED?

Your world was physically created after God first created the conceptual Adamic blueprint. Why? Because in order to sustain the physical bodies of the "sons of Adam," the earth had to be created first so that man could be put upon it. Do you see? God first created His goal, you, the Adamic man that is the concept of you. Before breathing life into this (concept) creation, He had to create the tools—the earth—so that your physical bodies could be sustained. You must prepare your "pot of dirt" before you can plant your seed. So God created His tools, the earth and all that is upon it, then He placed His created concept of Divine Man onto that world. In other words, He first created His goal through intent, then fashioned His tools, and then breathed life into His final creation.

We say to you here that you can do the same, for you are a spark of God. That divinity within you is the soil in which you plant your seed-goals, then water them to fruition with the glorious feeling of thanks and gratitude from your heart. That constant outpouring of gratitude is the "allowing" part of how to manifest—sustaining that higher vibratory level of faith in yourself as you live your life.

Remember, to strengthen your power, speak aloud. Bring your goal into your physical reality by the vibration of your voice. *That which you speak becomes concrete.* We do not mean for you to tell your goal to every passer-by; rather speak aloud in your meditations, your healing sessions with us, your walks in the park, your prayers. Your "outpouring" is really an "up-pouring!" The more you speak to Spirit, even though the room may seem empty, the closer you draw to us and draw us to you.

In order for you to ascend and live in the 5th dimension, the earth must first be prepared to receive you. Do you see the unfoldment of pattern here? The beautiful way in which God, in His Knowingness, has prepared All That Is to receive and support All That You Will Become? Please examine this last statement carefully, for it has many levels of meaning.

Just as this world was originally created to sustain your lives upon it, so must the earth ascend first, so that your 5D existence will be guaranteed to flourish. But since you are already here, living on earth, you are inextricably tied to the upward motion of her climb. For those of you awakened and aware, you can feel the changes all around you, inside and out, maybe still just beyond your ken [channeled December 2002]. We urge you to clear yourselves now! Once the earth finishes her transition, it will be much more difficult for you to blend into the higher levels of energy if you are still carrying imbalances, blockages and baggage from the lower dimensions. Those who are not aware will also be affected by the earth's ascension. They will unconsciously adjust, or deem it time to leave their bodies and return Home. All paths lead Home. All Be-ings reunite. Do not grieve too much, for you will find your loved ones sooner than you think!

If you find all of these patterns and levels too confusing or unwieldy, do not worry. Focus on preparing yourself, and leave the rest to Spirit. That is why we stress, over and over, the need to do the Circle of Grace. This self-clearing mechanism is in your body, has always been there, and has helped you to survive and grow. Now you have a great advantage— conscious awareness of your internal clearing process—through which you can accelerate your healing and gain mastery over your life.

YOUR BEST SPIRITUAL TOOL IS YOU!

The key that unlocks the door to the higher realms is not a physical key—it is a vibrational key! It is you, dear human, with all layers of your energetic being cleared, balanced and working in harmony. You must "key into" a higher level of harmony in order to reach us! Here we offer a recapitulation of the steps necessary to wield the Universal Law Of Allowing.

Step One: You materialize into your reality that which you focus on.

Step Two: You materialize what you focus on through an act of allowing your will to be done. How?
Imagine it done, keep giving thanks, and get busy collecting your tools.

Step Three: Knowing in the depths of your Be-ing that it is done is enough to bring in your goal and make it real. Simply sustain that "knowing" as you get ready to receive.

How to receive? Get busy creating those tools that your future self will need to wield after your goal is realized. You are your own best tool. How to begin? Begin by balancing all aspects of your energetic being through the Circle of Grace. Achieve a melding of all aspects, which puts your spiritual layer (and soon your Higher Self) in charge of your body and your life.

So, are you thinking, "Easy to say, hard to do"? Actually, you need "do" nothing physical except to will that your will be done! Your will resides in your etheric self, which is inextricably tied into your body. Wielding your will requires that you use your entire "Be-ing," both physical and auric, together! The physical root of your will lies deep within your solar plexus. To reach it, you must dive deep and draw it up with your visualization of what you want. That is the physical part. In order to send it up to Spirit, you must pull it up through your heart chakra, yes, with the emotional fuel of loving gratitude that will shoot it, straight and true, up into the higher realms of materialization.

This is called "bridging the dimensions," and this process will teach you to live in, and function from, the expanded reality that you seek. The true point of this teaching is not to reward you with a car, a better job, or any single tangible goal, though these things will come to you once you learn how to wield the universal laws. With the Circle of Grace work, we hope to facilitate your reaching your ultimate goal—becoming One with All That Is, at all levels. Once you reach that sacred space, dear one, the things that you will wish to materialize will be far different than your current list of wants or needs.

Remember we said that your entire energetic being resides on many planes of existence at once? Up until recently, you were only consciously aware of the 3D plane because that was the only dimension your physical senses could register. Remember the dog whistle? Dogs can hear an octave above you. Now that you are in 4D, we exist only an octave above you! As you "allow" all the aspects of your total Be-ing to work together, you achieve the full reconnection to Spirit you are seeking—communion with your own Higher Self. You need no longer work only from blind faith, dear one, your expanded awareness will give you new eyes, a new perspective, and a new level of power from which to create what you want.

What is your best tool for manifestation? It is your own energetic Be-ing, with all aspects cleared and functioning in smooth balance. That balance is under the direction of your spiritual layer, and can be attained through the regular use of the Circle of Grace. Do you see why we have stepped forward with the Circle of Grace healing information at this pivotal time of human evolution? The Veil of Forgetfulness is thinning, and you need to prepare for life beyond it. You will be living in many dimensions at once, beyond your current reality in 4D. As you expand your mental and spiritual awareness, realize that your body must also make that journey. Begin merging all that you have learned with the foundation of your being—your physical core. Begin your true journey upward with the Circle of Grace.

The Circle of Grace exercise is the path to clearing and balancing all aspects of your Be-ing to allow you to reach your highest potential. Study and learn, yes, and conceptualize all of those lessons into the expanded framework of thought that we offer you here. The true learning lies in the doing. Again, we say, you must clear and balance all aspects of self to become the perfect tool of God's will that your soul intends for you to be.

What are you meant to be? God's presence on earth. You are here so that all of your experiences and lessons will help you evolve back into the Godhead. Learn, yes, to prepare the tools you need. Do the work, yes, so that you will become the tool your own Higher Self needs, and that we in Spirit need for the full fruition of the Divine Plan. You are such small, heavily laden, yet valiant warriors, our own front lines, the ones "down in the dirt." That dirt is the precious body of Mother Earth, and you are her precious children, hers and ours, a holy meld of the blood and spirit of Father/Mother God.

We ask that you remember who you really are. To re-member is to re-join. Do you see the layers of meaning in those words? We wait impatiently for our re-union with you, for we miss you greatly. That is also why we are here and endeavor to merge with you, to help you ascend gracefully to our level of existence. Please remember that, while your human lives are short, your true existence is eternal.

You spend most of your time in the True Reality of Spirit, as an eternal Be-ing. Your lesson time in each body is relatively short in comparison. You are already "One with Us," you just don't remember. It is in this incredible time, this short window of ascension, that we offer you the choice to rejoin us while still in body. You need not die, as you understand death. You never cease to exist; on the contrary, your true spiritual reality is put on hold while you are away, in body and in lesson.

Your progress up the metaphysical path is predicated upon your dedication. We do not ask you to spend hours in contemplation or change your life to accommodate these directions. Rather, we ask you to take care of yourselves, for you are all precious to us, every single one. We act here as facilitators to smooth your path, to offer you guidance and hope. Even more, we offer you Spirit help if you will only seek it. Be patient with us as we teach you how to clear yourself, how to reach within and find the spark of divinity that is the core truth of your soul. It is an exciting inward journey, an adventure that you share, alone, with Spirit.

We are always near, and you are always dear.

You will find a need to reread this material. Different things will come forth to your attention each time. We teach in layers upon layers, as is the nature of all existence. We say to you that you are ready to shed a layer and reach up for a new one. You need to be prepared for the journey, and plan a map of where you see your destination to be. We can help you with both of these things, by teaching you the way things work in the higher realms.

You will then know how to make the universal laws work for you!

To accomplish all of this, you must seek a balance within your life that will accommodate both your quest for health and your quest for spirituality. Sit down and evaluate your life, really look at the division of your time, your energy and your focus. Most people have a true imbalance between work and play—too much work, too little play. Play is a form of rest. Rest is not just lying down, but also doing things that feed your soul, or rest your brain or comfort your senses. If you feel the need to work incessantly, ask yourself, why? Do you truly need a bigger house or another car, or do you truly need some time off to recover your energy and your enthusiasm for life?

All of these steps lead you back to merging with Spirit, to going Home. We ask that you consider this very important point: *The true value of your existence lies in the journey.* Enjoy your life. See the glass as always half full, find your bliss in every breath and in every moment.

You are in charge of your life. Begin to nourish that truth inside of yourself, in order to manifest your divine birthright. It is time to step off of the karmic wheel and gain a new, strong, steadfast foothold back in the world which is your True Reality. Once your 4D world rises far enough in frequency to begin blending with our 5D world, you will have arrived! We wait impatiently for that moment, even as we create it together. We yearn for your Homecoming, our splendid reunion with you in the True Reality of Spirit.

Chapter Eight

The Law of Divine Creation

I AM GOD • YOU ARE GOD • WE ARE ONE

In this chapter, we would like to focus on another universal law. We have already covered the Law of Materialization in Chapter Six, which explains how to materialize into your reality that which you focus on. The Law Of Allowing, Chapter Seven, teaches you how to allow into your world that which you focus on and desire from the depths of your heart.

Here we wish to discuss the ultimate universal law: Belief in One God. It is also called the Law Of Divine Creation. This law simply states that, indeed, All Is One. That means We are all One, and you as humans are part of that "We." Therefore, if you are part of All That Is, you have those same characteristics as God, with the same basic morals that govern all life but, most important, you have the power within you to create as God does.

The crowning gift from Spirit to humanity is the inherent birthright to be all that God is. That is the whole point of the ascension process, rejoining All That Is while a piece of your soul awareness inhabits a human body. And that will be man's crowning glory, to become a bridge between dimensions, between different levels of consciousness, to return to Spirit without dying and leaving the body.

Do you see why your entire being must be ready, at all levels, to make this leap? Being emotionally, mentally and spiritually awakened is wonderful progress, but will only take you three-quarters of the way up the spiritual path. You must be cleared and balanced in body, as well, to fully actualize the goal. To that end, we have stepped forward to explain how things really work and to offer our aid in your journey back to self-realization.

The Brotherhood's dedication of effort to the Divine Plan is to help humanity to evolve. So, you see, in addition to being essential for your progress, our "collaboration," if you will, serves to help us do our chosen work, too. And our chosen work here, dear ones, is to bring into your awareness the Circle of Grace.

The Circle of Grace is a comprehensive exercise that clears, balances and integrates all levels of your true Be-ing. There are many Brothers waiting to be called upon for help, more than there are humans on the planet. As we exist in the Now of circular time, we are available to you each and every time you call upon us. For those of you reaching and seeking, yet not finding synchronicity, we say to you, Be that which you studied. Become, physically, an expression of All Love. Work past your fears and doubts, clear yourselves so that you may become the instrument of God's plan that you chose to be in this life before it began, while you were still among us in Spirit.

Those of you who lie down and seek our help will find us.

Within this body of text are embedded many layers of information, in the explanation of the form and function of the True Reality that you cannot yet see. As you make progress, you will find new information that shines forth from rereading the text. There are answers to all of your questions as well, regarding the Circle of Grace exercise and how to do it. We, the Brotherhood of Light, offer you our help, if you seek it. If you have trouble connecting with our energy, simply begin reading any passage and we will come in through the frequency of the written text.

We have endeavored to teach you how to clear and balance all the layers of your body, both physical and etheric. At the end of the Circle of Grace explanation, we told you that the spiritual layer governs all of the other layers, and that all layers must work together in a clear and balanced union. Now, at the end of the section on universal laws, we say to you that all of the preceding laws depend and rely on the total assimilation of this law: the Law of Divine Creation. *Do you see that in order to manipulate your reality to create what you want, you must, above all, believe that you can do it?*

Both the Law of Materialization and the Law of Allowing can only function for you if you believe in your own power. In other words, you must wield all three universal laws together. They work in order thusly: Know that you are the Divine Creator. Define your goal with precise focus. Refine your goal as you make room for it to come in. Again, we point out, there are circles within circles of cause and effect. Knowing how to cause that effect allows you to will it into being. This power comes within your reach when you understand how to work with, and within, the laws of the universe. In other words, the Law of Divine Creation is the seat of your will. The Laws of Materialization and Allowing explain how to wield your will.

Remember this: When you wield your will as Divine Creator, you are creating a frequency change around you. All of life is defined by vibratory patterns that then translate into physicality. You are changing the vibratory blueprint of your future—your creation of a goal begins at the etheric level. That is how God creates, and that is what you are learning to do.

As Jesus said, "All that I do, you can do also." Once you fully believe, down to your very biology, that all of this is possible, then it will be possible. You have incredible spiritual (etheric) powers that you are simply not aware of. There are those among you who have succeeded at great levels in the material world; all of them focused forcefully on what they wanted in order to achieve their goals. The price of power in your society is indeed, overwork, illness and dysfunctional families. That used to be what it took—total and full focus for many life-times—to achieve any mastery toward ascension.

Now, time is "growing short," as you say, and you are feeling the effects of its compression. There is a compression, then a null zone, then comes the compression of the next, higher dimensional frequency. Once you rise fully into the "vibrational band" of 5D, then the energy will even out, balancing you and everything around you to this new, higher level. That is when we will finally, fully meet. Remember, all dimensions exist in the same space, separated by bands of frequency. Those people who remain unenlightened and unaware will remain in 3D. What they won't know is simply this: *3D and 4D are included in 5D.*

You have come a long way in your understanding of meta- physics in a very short period of time (linear time as you know it) since the mid-1980s. There is now an ever-rising exponential curve of new awakenings, as more and more people become aware that there is something more to life and begin to seek the Light. We ask that you continue to put your focus and energy into your upward, inward climb, and gently say that in order to do this well, you must conserve your energies and stop wasting them. It is you, first-awakened, who will help the mass- es to follow a new path, one that you create with every step that you take in your spiritual quest for wholeness and balance.

In this time of global strife, do you finally see clearly the waste of energy and life that comes from arguing over whose God is better? There is only one God. We repeat, *There is only one totality of consciousness that constructs and directs all of the many universes that comprise the body of All That Is.*

The Brotherhood of Light is composed of many different life expressions, yet we all work together. Do you see this as an example? If we warred amongst ourselves as to who is better, who knows more and who is closer to God's truth, the Brotherhood and all that it stands for would be destroyed, and justly so. Then we could not fulfill our major chosen func- tion—helping humanity to evolve. That is why we come in as the Brothers and do not identify ourselves as individuals. Our work with you is what is most important, not who we each are.

Know that for each person, event and situation, the appro- priate Brothers will step forward to help. As we are all One, so are you all One with Us. As we help you to ascend, you help us to ascend, too. As each level rises, the levels above and below must necessarily rise, as well. That is the Divine Plan, and we all play a part in it, each in our own way.

The concept of All Is One includes the following axioms: All Is As It Should Be; believe in Me, and so believe in life eternal; turn thine eyes up to the heavens, and you will find yourselves, and Me, in the same moment. We speak to you as the voice of God's Brotherhood, the Brotherhood of Light, one of the many faces of God.

We are all a part of All That Is, you and us. Listening to the inner voice of your consciousness (or conscience) is listening to Higher Self, to higher truth. In order to rise gracefully with the heightening energies, we offer this advice: Go forth and be guided by the strength of your intuitive feelings—that which is good will feel good and right. That which is bad will feel bad and you will recognize it as such, even if it gives you momentary pleasure. Your inner heart will always guide you true, though your mind and the mind-set of others may disagree. Remember that your divine power lies in wielding your positive emotions through your heart—that is the creative power of love. Negative emotions drag you back down to lower frequencies, causing you to miscreate through negative intent. Learn to recognize the difference, and choose wisely!

There will be more external strife and stress as you work your way through this pivotal time in human history [channeled February 2003]. Keep peace in your heart, no matter what goes on around you. Both your local and global problems represent life lessons, in graduating levels of understanding, levels of learning and levels of advancement. They all serve to bring you Home again, with the clear and sure knowledge that God exists, and that God exists for all. Not for some, but for all.

Do you follow?

We hope you will, for there is only one true path Home, and that is through the Heart.

THE VOICE OF I AM SPEAKS

The heart of man will reach up and connect with the Heart of God, and you will know when that occurs, yes, you will! Yes, children, you will know, for then I will appear to you, to each one in his right time and place, for you are all beloved. Darkness was only created for the purpose of making My

Light shine more brightly. Evil is the same—a countermirror to
Love. Have you not suffered enough? Have you not learned
enough? I ask that you find your way Home through love and
kindness, so that We may, once again, all consciously reside
together in the body of All That Is.

When you reach upward and pray, "Dear Lord,
Father/Mother God, Creator of all that is, was, and ever will
be," do you see the totality of that prayer? The wholeness of
that prayer? The wonder of being part of All That Is? I cherish
you all, and it is time for you to cherish Me in the same way
that I cherish you. I give you this image: If you could all, every
last man, woman and child, lay down your weapons of war and
embrace love, then you will all ascend, in that first split-second
of total Brotherhood of Man. Then, truly, you will have created
Eden in your midst, by eradicating evil, anger and hatred in
your hearts. Those of you who choose to go home will, in that
instant, be brought Home to Me. Those of you who choose to
stay, and live in the higher realities that you have created, will
rejoice in every breath and every day that you spend on your
beautiful planet. That will be your "New Jerusalem," the bright
future of earth that metaphysics offers.

In the Law of Divine Creation, I say this to you:

I Am One • You Are One • We Are One

It is sad and wasteful for you to fight over whose image of
Me is better. I wish for no man to kill another, for all life is
precious. I say to you: Now is the time for Global
Brotherhood. Now is the time for all of Man to unite as brothers under the skin and direct your energies and passions
towards more useful purposes. Work on eradicating hunger,
poverty and, most of all, ignorance, anger and fear. If you feel
the need to defend yourselves against "evil" in your reality, so
be it. Evil only exists as a mirror to Good. That which is Good
will always prevail. That which is evil cannot, and will not, win.

Dear ones, there is no such thing as "hell." Those whom you
perceive as evil, even if they have done grievous harm, come
back to Me after their lives are over. I judge no one, but rather
give you the right to judge your own progress after each life.
Your "evil doers" are also part of the Divine Plan in the sense

that they have agreed to a difficult life path, taking on a contract that stipulates that they create evil, fear and horror as lessons to teach humanity.

To teach you what? To teach you that all life is precious. To teach you that *all forms of life are equally precious*. To teach you that all that is, is really All That Is. These lessons are still being processed and must be played out in your material world, even though many of you have superceded the need for it at the spiritual level.

These teachings must be assimilated at all levels, including the physical. The Circle of Grace is a process that will help you assimilate your lessons at the individual, cellular level. The Global Brotherhood of Man is the necessary manifestation of this very same clearing process, played out at the global physical level. Why is this needed? It must all go together, children, it can only work when the smallest detail has been covered, when all levels shift together, from deep inside the earth to the outer reaches of your galaxy and beyond.

When one level shifts, all levels must shift.

This lesson is a repetition and expansion of your Second World War, in which six million of My children offered up their lives to show man the stupidity of hatred and the sadness of racism. Though many of you did learn, many soon forgot. Some even argued that it never actually happened. I do not judge what stand you take; you must each come to your own personal understanding of right and wrong, good and evil, God vs. No God. For Catholics to fight Protestants is not right. I represent all, and I love you all. For China against Tibet, for Russia against Kosovo, for India against Pakistan, for Palestinian against Jew, I say to all of you the same thing: *Please, stop now.* Realize that your fighting and killing is not the true way of God. You gain nothing, until you learn the lessons involved. You will see victory, perhaps, but it will be empty of true meaning and worth.

As Global Man, your victory is assured as soon as all the fighting stops. As each of you individually works on your personal ascension, you fuel the ascension of all humanity. The true victory of humanity is living harmoniously together, when all men release the need to kill. Once you achieve a firm foothold in the higher realms, killing will be abhorrent to you, for it goes against the Will Of God. Once you feel My presence as a living force within you, you will not want to kill! Then your reality will change, the planet will change, and you will have no need for war. Peace will loom large all around the earth, when enough of you are finally One with Me.

You have lived many, many lifetimes in order to come back to your original state of Oneness with God. It is time to assimilate your lessons, to learn and grow and move on as a species, as a Global Brotherhood, as a human expression of God In Action. It is time for you to move past those lessons, and begin to live the ultimate truth: You are all One. How many more deaths will it take for you to learn this? How many more deaths will it take before you stop killing each other and start helping each other?

I say to you, it is far easier, far simpler, and requires less energy to love rather than to hate. The laying down of hatred in your lives is an act of allowing love to shine forth in your hearts. That is why I have, through the words of the Brothers, endeavored to give you My teachings, My path for you to follow in order to come back Home to Me.

I Am God. I Am the Brotherhood.
I Am All That Is and You Are Part of Me.
Do you follow?
I hope you will.

For this is an act of will that I require, an act of free will, to release fear in all of its faces in your lives and embrace the one truth that I represent: *Unconditional Love.*

It is so simple, and so close to you. Reach out to each other, and thus you will be reaching up to Me. Do I favor one color of skin over another? Never. I created you all, different yet equal. Do I favor one form of religion over another? Never.

I Am One. It is you who have created these divisions. It is you who must now erase that hatred from your hearts, and heal those divisions so that you can all come together, and create *love* all around your globe. The moment that you do this, the instant that you accomplish this, your graduation and your return Home will be guaranteed.

I wish to comment on the word "will." I ask that you reread this material, and see how many times, and in how many ways, the word "will" was used. It is a pattern, a trigger, a path to lead you to your own understanding that you are in charge of your lives, your will to make it what it is, for better or worse. Are not those words used in your marriage ceremonies, "...for better or worse, in sickness and health, till death do us part"? Yes, now look at that phrase again, and see the marriage that I offer you here. I love you and cherish you and welcome you back, no matter what state you are in—better or worse, sick or healthy. *Death reunites Us, dear ones.* Your translation back to the realm of Spirit is your true Homecoming, while your birth into body has been, up until now, your separation from the True Reality that I represent.

I send you forth to learn these lessons, that you may come back to Me in the purity of love. I ask only that you find within yourselves the purity of love from which you sprang. Then all of your lifetimes, all of your wisdom and knowledge gained, I will assimilate into My Body, that I may, too, learn and grow from you. Do you see the Circle of Grace at work here? It is the unending fountain of universal energy that I placed within you, to guide you Home.

I Am That I Am. You are of Me, and to Me you shall return. Until then, I await you in the quiet silence of your own inner truth, in the energetic cycle of healing and clearing that I bestowed to your bodies when I created you. Do you think that I would neglect your care? I care for you, and I reach for you; whenever you close your eyes and sleep, I heal and cleanse you from within.

Now, in this time of great transition, I bring this knowledge, this precious information, before the Veil. The Circle of Grace is your way Home. I bring it into the light so that you may see it, understand it, use it and, in so doing, come Home to Me. I give you this blessing, and the clarity of understanding it through the efforts of the Brotherhood of Light, so that your path will be clearly lit. Even look at the name of the Brotherhood of Light—it represents all that *I Am*, all that I stand for, and all that I require of you, to become brothers in the light of day, in the light of love, in the Light and Love of God. I ask that you pay attention now, all of my children, and see that, indeed, you are all one family, representing all of the Oneness that *I Am*.

Why did I create you thus? To give you more opportunity to learn and grow. Are there not a myriad different trees and plants on earth? Different species of birds and animals on earth? Each one of you plays a part and has a specific role in the grand plan that I have created. There is a specific purpose to the dolphin, and to the whale and to the shark. I ask that you honor all forms of life on your planet, at every level of creation. Stop killing each other. Stop killing My beloved crawling and flying and swimming creatures. Stop destroying this beautiful world that I created for you—do you not see the layers of pattern, the circles within circles that encapsulate all of life? You cannot willfully destroy an aspect or area of life on earth without the entire life cycle of the planet being affected. I ask that you look beyond your needs of the moment and become the caretakers of this living planet that you were meant to be. I ask you to look to the needs of the earth and tend to her, for she is truly your physical mother. The more you connect with the earth, the easier will be your rising along with her.

So, my dear children, it is time. Now is the time of special dispensation. Now is the emergence of Spirit's True Reality, and I ask that you listen to Me now. You are so close, and yet many of you still harbor doubt. Do you not see Me in the perfection of the smallest detail, in the wonder of every form of life? All of the Divine Plan is balanced, from the smallest form to the highest form, to return to Me. That is your primary goal, the goal of each and every lifetime. I have told you how to create it. Now it is up to you to do so.

Do you follow?

I Hope You Will.

I Am, in All Love, All That Is You.

Chapter Nine

The Completion: Healing Your Life

<u>All Of Life Is A Circle</u>
That which you now pretend,
You will Be in the end.
The end is a new beginning,
That is the way of Eternal Beings.
Do the Circle of Grace with us,
And find your way back to Godliness.

I t is no accident that this is the ninth and final chapter—
nine is the number of completion. We commend you for
having read this far! Each step is honored, dear ones, no
matter the size.

Through this work, and through our work together in the
Circle of Grace process, we hope to aid you up the ladder of
evolution, your evolution from the limited existence you have
experienced up until now while in human form. A new form of
human is rising up—and it is the rising up that creates the new
form (chuckle). We await impatiently for you to call us in, so
that we may begin to walk up that road together.

Have you learned what all of your God-given gifts are? The
power of intent, plus will, plus universal energy moving
through the body in the Circle of Grace, will bring you
through healing into spiritual harmony. What is that? Why, all
of your layers blended and singing together to form the unique

chord of your spiritual essence. That which is the Eternal You will soon walk with the human you on earth.

Once enough of the population has evolved, the dynamics of the human consciousness will be forever changed. But know that your work had to come first, in order to raise human awareness enough so that the needs of the many will become most important. You will then outgrow the need for war and fighting. Why? Because you will have outgrown the need to continue feeding the karmic engine of your 3D duality. Oh, then the tides will turn, children, and you lightworkers will be much needed. That is why we are here, for you, for those who seek to know and learn and grow. For those who know that there is more to life, who know that there must be more to life than what is apparent, to make it all worthwhile and meaningful.

Did you not often wonder why people were born only to grow old and die? Those of you who said, "This is a colossal waste of energy with no point," were called crazy by everyone else! But if you overlay the grander plan of Spirit over these endlessly repeating lives (as some of your oldest religions do) then it all begins to make sense. If you realize that each life earns you love and wisdom, each life brings you a step or two closer to remerging with God, would that not be worthwhile? Would it not make more sense?

We are not trying to convert you here to our mode of beliefs (chuckle), but merely to point out that being part of a glorious Divine Plan makes a lot of the "bad stuff" more bearable. It allows you to clearly see the true shape of your lessons. What once were huge obstacles in your life will become temporary delays! Simply put, once you identify a lesson you can complete it and move beyond...up the path toward Home.

Life is harder, dear ones, for those of you who are fixed in duality, who have given up believing that there is a God at all. Why? Because *You and God Are One*. To deny the existence of God is to deny your own self-worth. *You are so much more powerful than you know!* So, if you resonate with these words, this information and this exercise, it is no accident that you are, indeed, reading this book. It will be no accident when you lie down and do the Circle of Grace and feel our presence.

Are you aware, by now, that there is no such thing as coincidence? That accidents don't just happen? That luck is being prepared when opportunity presents itself? Your journey can be as simple or as complex as you make it. The choice is always yours. Though certain things have been predetermined, yes, those things were chosen also by you, at the soul contract level before you came in to this current life. So even those aspects of your life that seem like destiny or fate, both of which obviate the necessity of your taking responsibility for it, are really still yours to own and control. Once you realize this, and know that you are in full charge of your life, then you have the power to control it.

You have the power to create anything that you desire or require.

That is the meaning and the power behind the phrase, You Are God.

We wish to clearly state here: God Is All. You Are God. We Are God. We are All One. Therefore:

You have the power of Infinite Creation.

Taking on God's mantle and being One with God is your goal here and now. Some of you will step into that reality one day, in a split second it will hit you for sure that, "All Is As It Should Be." That is when you will know, beyond a shadow of a doubt, that God exists everywhere, in everything, including within you. Most of you need to expand your mental framework of reference and absorb all the concepts of metaphysics before you can incorporate them into your lives. There are always lessons within lessons within lessons. Nothing is as simple as it appears to be, and yet simplicity is what you should all strive for. If this sounds paradoxical, then we say that paradoxes are also lessons!

Just as your body is always fighting off germs and occasionally gets sick, this cycle serves to strengthen the immune system. Next time you catch a cold, think of how it is helping your health! A paradox? Yes, but that is how the body works. It needs to be challenged and taxed, within reason, to stay balanced and healthy. How? By being put off balance and having to regain balance. Had you not developed resistance to germs in your environment, the human race would have quickly died out. Similarly, your body—at all levels—needs clearing and balancing to stay whole and healthy. Circles within circles!

In the same way, life serves you up lessons to strengthen you physically, emotionally, mentally and spiritually. Do you recognize these layers by now? Yes, they are the layers of your true, total Be-ing. In the same way that your body represents the microcosm of the macrocosm, so do you, too, each and every human being, represent God in physical embodiment. Do you see the layers? Does it not make you smile, the complex simplicity of God's consciousness?

One of the things that we will remind you to do in our healing sessions together is bring us your conceptual problems, so that we may help you assimilate this new information at all levels. Part of total healing requires that you become Godlike, to embark each day in that mental state of waking meditation that is a merging, a blending of all of the dimensions into which you are growing. In order to become a blended being, one that walks in conscious connection with Higher Self, you must fully understand, digest and function in the new energy.

In the healing of your bodies and the assimilation of your divine birthright you are creating a new, evolved paradigm of the human being. God is very pleased, children, to see you thus learn and grow. We, the Brothers, are humbled to be a part of this process, and to be working with you magnificent Be-ings. Some of us have shared incarnations with you, and some of us have never served time on earth. It matters not, as long as we all contribute our talents and devotion to the Divine Plan, as you are doing in your everyday life.

Though you may not be consciously aware that you made this choice, if you are present in body at this time in human history, then you signed up for this last and first life as evolving Be-ings. That was your goal back in Spirit, when you chose this life and then piled on top of it all the lessons you had left to learn! Yes, dear ones, you still have some clearing to do but, in retrospect, in this current life you are clearing more than the last hundred lifetimes put together. Your work with us within the Circle Of Grace will serve to move you forward quickly on the path back to self-realization, back to Higher Self awareness, back to God.

There will soon come a time when this new energy, the refined frequencies of the higher dimensions, will lock in all over the planet. Remember, it is earth's ascension, children; you are along for the ride. What will that bring? Heaven is a state of consciousness that you can achieve while still in body. Be-ing in 5D is like being in Heaven, from a 3D perspective. But from that 3D perspective also came the separation of man from Heaven, and you thought your body had to die before your spirit would be released and returned to God. As you think, so it is, and so it has been for thousands of your earth years' history.

All of that no longer applies, children. There are new rules in 5D, new ideas, new strength, new support, new love from God that you will all feel directly. Then you will know, beyond any question, that you are a part of God, have always been and will always be a part of God. We offer you another image here to help you see your divinity, to see yourselves as having moved through and beyond your lessons: Take all of your experiences learned from, and stack them as a broad foundation that you stand squarely upon, legs as towers of strength, torso as one big heart representing your truest wish, arms held up to the skies to direct the flight of your prayer to its target, head held proud and tall to be the crowning glory of God In Man, and eyes closed to the minor outside reality so that you may focus on the magnificent inner reality that you carry within.

We strive to give you a picture here, of you standing huge and tall, connecting Mother Earth to Father Sky. Connect the precious dirt beneath your feet to your glorious ascent into the heavenly skies. You are the connection between earth and God. Through your physical transmutation from 3D human to 5D human, you will connect Spirit's ascension to the planet's earthly ascension. You are the catalysts, brave volunteers that took on the task of being the glue between Spirit and matter, by coming in as living creatures that represent both. As you progress in your spiritual transformation of matter—for that is what you are doing—the frequency changes you create will affect all levels, all dimensions, all of life everywhere. Why?

We Are All One. We are all Brothers in the Divine Plan, working for the expansion and edification of All That Is. This time in human history, brief as it is, is a huge window of opportunity for each and every soul now on earth. If you are here, your soul wanted to be here.

And we await you, with celebration in our hearts, for no matter what happens you will return to the higher realms. *You are Eternal, remember?* Death is a transition back to True Reality, and is no more than that. Fear of death, as all fear, comes from ignorance, comes from not knowing what lies beyond. It is only because of the Veil of Forgetfulness that you have built up such negativity around death. So many of you have distanced yourselves from that part of the life process that growing old and dying has become a shameful, ugly thing, not to be watched or felt too closely. This, we find sad. Yet it is just a mind-set, and mind-sets can be changed, improved and refined.

We ask that you care for your dying relatives and help them through the door back to Spirit with lighter hearts, dear ones. Look towards the reunion, not the separation. Again, it is a question of perspective. When you cannot change a situation, you can change your perspective of it, and in doing so change the energy of that situation and how it plays out. Can you see the need to honor those souls who are leaving as much as you honor those coming in? You will all be together soon enough, for *nobody really dies!* And be heartened, children, there is no hell except for in your expectations. You create what you focus on, remember?

We hope that this material will help your progress up the path to self-mastery. Many of you are further along than you think, and many more are awakening at an earlier age. Time as you know it grows short. Time as we know it is endless. This, too, you will come to understand.

How do you know when you have reached Selfhood? When it no longer matters!

When you no longer feel ego attachment, then you are developing spiritual discernment. You will find yourself standing witness to other peoples' lessons, seeing their "maya" or "drama" for what it truly is—the acting out of lessons in the physical earth reality of 3D. In your current Now of 4D, you are learning to identify and move beyond those lessons. When you can see this happening all around you, identify it for what it is *and not react to it*, you will be perceiving life from 5D. You will know when that happens, dear ones, you will most certainly know!

Of all of the steps needed for the Divine Plan to unfold, this step, this willful evolution of mind over matter, is one of the hardest to achieve. We honor humanity greatly for the burdens you have shouldered, time after time, to move the karmic wheel forward. It is now time to step off of it, and stride back to the True Reality of Spirit with no more need for karma and no more need for the Veil of Forgetfulness. This is, truly, a monumental achievement!

Once you have achieved blending with your Higher Self, what then? What will you do? We hope that you will stay in body, and shine your ascended light on all who draw near. We will guide and support you in a concrete way because you will have concrete communication with the higher realms. Once you are fully in the flow of the new energy, your shining light will be that of unconditional love, God-love.

God loves all things, great and small.

You, too, will find room in you heart to love all of creation, once you are cleared and balanced to the new frequencies. Time will become merely a staircase which you will use to get where you want to go. Your senses, your talents and your gifts will unfurl. Your life will become healed and balanced, as you become the healed and balanced masters of your co-creative reality. Start now, children, start wielding those universal laws. Pretend that you are already self-realized, each time you lie down and reach up for our help through the Circle of Grace. Pretend that you are already healed, already tuned in, already joined to Spirit, for, indeed, you already are One with us. Can you not see our words before you?

We wish to end this tome with one simple question, one that is already in your present-day framework of reference. Overlay this question on your future creations and shape them with the loving support of Spirit. It is simply this:

**If you knew that you could not fail,
what would you do with your life?**

Do you follow?
We hope you will!

We await You, In All Love, Your Brotherhood of Light.

Mission Statement

The human consciousness is rising very quickly into higher awareness, and the energetic changes on planet Earth in the next decade will overwhelm many of us. In addition to helping people to help themselves, the Brotherhood's *Circle of Grace* will help bring holistic modalities together to work in synchronicity. Learning to release pain and stress from the meridians of our nervous systems is key to healing our lives at all levels. *All holistic modalities can be applied to this natural clearing process we have within our bodies.*

Lightworkers, it is essential to pool our talents and tools in order to help the masses shift. No matter what methodology you use, know that *The Circle of Grace* process releases fear from our bodies, allowing room for love. By clearing imbalances, we raise our energetic vibration to a place where we can and will work miracles.

The core goal of the Brotherhood of Light is to facilitate the ascension of humanity. They offer their knowledge of healing and of higher concepts to further our integration of science and spirituality, physics and metaphysics, alternative healing and allopathic medicine. The Brothers focus on teaching us how to heal our entire Be-ing, including the physical body. This will empower us to reach self-mastery and consciously connect us all back to Spirit. Then we will truly become the Global Brotherhood of Man.

I Am, in All Love, Edna G. Frankel (Sara)

Medical Disclaimer: Information in
this book is intended to support and
supplement current medical
practices. If you have a physical
illness, please consult your doctor.

Author's Note: "The Brotherhood of Light" was the title Spirit
chose to call its voice in 1990 when I entered into active meditation
with them. The Brothers' original name is the Order of Melchizedek.
In our history, we have also called them the White Brotherhood and
the Great White Brotherhood. I just call them "the Bros." I had a ton
of questions and found that they have infinite patience. See where ask -
ing the right questions can lead you?

At first, they called me "little Brother." When I pointed out that I
was female in this life (dualistic chuckle), they gave me the gift of my
Spirit name, Sara, formed from the first two and last two letters of my
Higher Self's name, Sanat Kumara. I work alone with the Brothers,
and see myself as their scribe and voice for information on healing at
all levels. I hold no affiliation with any person, group or organization
currently representing the Melchizedek or (Great) White Brotherhood
names.

About the Author

Edna G. Frankel was born in Cairo, Egypt, in 1954 to a French-speaking family of Romanian, Greek and Turkish descent. Evicted in the Suez Crisis of 1956, they immigrated to the United States in 1960. She was raised in New York City and attended the United Nations International School in Manhattan and then Washington University in St. Louis, Missouri. In addition to a B.A. in Psychology and a B.A. in French, she is also a certified free-lance editor.

Edna and her family live in suburban Philadelphia, Pennsylvania. Her daughter Lisa is at Harvard University's School of Divinity, pursuing a Master of Theological Studies degree. Her son Robbie is studying art and photography at Alfred University. Her three Siamese cats are all Reiki-attuned and sleep in a big, warm pile.

A full-time metaphysical channel and author, Edna G. Frankel is also a holistic teacher of Modern Reiki and The Circle of Grace clearing process. She began studying Usui Reiki in 1985, became a teaching Master in 1994, and has also studied Lightarian Reiki, Tummo Reiki, Sekhem-Seichem Reiki, Master Angelic Alignment and Reconnective HealingTM. In both her seminars and private practice, she incorporates the use of multiple modalities and energetic tools. She offers seminars on The Circle of Grace in Philadelphia, and at holistic and metaphysical conferences in the United States.

Edna does both private and public channeled sessions from the Brotherhood of Light and the Ascended Masters. All sessions are recorded; sometimes, general information is used as material for publication. Since May 2001, Edna has been a contributing author to the international monthly magazine *Sedona Journal Of Emergence!* Her channeled pieces also appear in the yearly series, *Predictions Book,* by Light Technology Publishing.

The current body of work being channeled from the Brotherhood, "Frequency & Physicality," began in September 2002. This new healing information explains how the Millennium Shift affects our bodies, and how to gracefully transition with the heightened incoming energies. Visit the "Published Articles" section at www.beyondreiki.com to read recent text from this new series!

To order copies of *The Circle of Grace*, please contact:

Edna G. Frankel
P.O. Box 62, Blue Bell, PA, 19422, USA
www.beyondreiki.com • ednagfrankel@aol.com

Volume discounts for metaphysical groups are available!